"We don't have to go looking for it. It will come and find us. Sooner or later, suffering at a catastrophic level will wreck our lives. Paul Tripp understands that personally. He also understands the gospel personally. His new book does not trivialize our sufferings with glib formulas. This wise book leads us deeper into the gospel of the cross and closer to the Man of Sorrows himself."

Ray Ortlund, Lead Pastor, Immanuel Church, Nashville, Tennessee

"This book is a balm to the soul that you will pick up and not be able to put down; it will also become a beloved friend to return to for years to come and trusted wisdom to pass out to other weary wanderers."

Ann Voskamp, *New York Times* best-selling author, *The Broken Way* and *One Thousand Gifts*

"Writing after the shock of unexpectedly losing his health and dealing with ongoing suffering, Paul Tripp offers very practical advice. In particular, his reflections on common 'traps' often faced by people who suffer will prove helpful to many who find themselves being tossed about by the storms of life."

Kelly M. Kapic, author, *Embodied Hope*; Professor of Theological Studies, Covenant College

"Dealing daily with quadriplegia and chronic pain (and having battled stage III cancer), I know something about suffering—and to be honest, there's hardly a book on the subject I haven't read. But when Paul David Tripp offers his insights on our afflictions, *that* gets my attention. And this book does not disappoint. Yes, Paul offers an empathetic ear and solid comfort, but he fills these pages with practical, no-nonsense counsel on how to move through and beyond suffering into a fresh and lively hope. I highly recommend this remarkable new work."

Joni Eareckson Tada, Founder and CEO, Joni and Friends International Disability Center

"I have read countless books on suffering, but few have inspired me to reevaluate my own adversity the way *Suffering* has. Paul Tripp's willingness to unpack his own pain, candidly sharing the insights he has gleaned, is an unspeakable gift. His personal story is both riveting and reassuring as it points us to the unshakable hope we have in Christ, even in unimaginable circumstances. This book is a masterpiece. I cannot recommend it highly enough."

Vaneetha Rendall Risner, author, *The Scars That Have Shaped Me: How God Meets Us in Suffering*

"Honest. Compelling. Grace filled. This book is a gift. Paul Tripp speaks to us not as a theoretician but as a fellow sufferer. His counsel is illuminated by personal experiences, informed by biblical truth, and infused with gospel hope. With compassion and empathy, he fortifies us against the common temptations we face when suffering and helps us see that our suffering, however great, was never meant to define us. Most importantly, he points us to the Savior who has suffered in our place so that we might be ever confident of his love, his wisdom, and his good purposes for our lives."

Bob Kauflin, Director, Sovereign Grace Music

"Once more, Paul Tripp has taken God's truth and applied it to our souls in a way that is both challenging and comforting. He understands the deep wells of suffering from his own experience and that of others he counsels. He clearly identifies the tempting traps that so frequently entice the heart of the sufferer, then beckons him on to find rest in God. This book will be my 'go-to' to give those looking to understand God's good work of suffering in our lives. I am so sorry for Tripp's suffering, but I am so grateful for this book!"

Connie Dever, author, *He Will Hold Me Fast*; Curriculum and Music Writer, The Praise Factory

"Paul Tripp writes this book with an honesty and humility that invites us into God's intimate work on his heart through the dark nights. What he found—and what you'll find if you read this book—is that the gospel of Jesus Christ brings us hope even in the most confusing and painful moments of life. Whether or not you're suffering today, read this book and prepare yourself for the days ahead."

Dave Furman, Senior Pastor, Redeemer Church of Dubai; author, *Kiss the Wave* and *Being There*

"Paul Tripp always writes with honesty, authenticity, and gospel sanity. But in this new book, Paul gifts us with a vulnerability that is rare, freeing, and inviting. As he chronicles his own journey through a life-threatening illness, Tripp helps us understand the difference between hope and hype—between spiritual spin and trusting our Father when our control, dignity, and certainty are under assault. This is one of the most timely, courageous, and helpful books on suffering I have ever read."

Scotty Ward Smith, Pastor Emeritus, Christ Community Church, Franklin, Tennessee; Teacher in Residence, West End Community Church, Nashville, Tennessee

Suffering

Suffering

Gospel Hope When Life Doesn't Make Sense

PAUL DAVID TRIPP

 **CROSSWAY**®

WHEATON, ILLINOIS

Cover design: Tyler Deeb, Misc. Goods Co.

First printing 2018

Printed in the United States of America

Scripture quotations are from the ESV® Bible (The Holy Bible, English Standard Version®), copyright © 2001 by Crossway, a publishing ministry of Good News Publishers. Used by permission. All rights reserved.

Hardcover ISBN: 978-1-4335-5677-7
ePub ISBN: 978-1-4335-5680-7
PDF ISBN: 978-1-4335-5678-4
Mobipocket ISBN: 978-1-4335-5679-1

Library of Congress Cataloging-in-Publication Data

Names: Tripp, Paul David, 1950- author.
Title: Suffering : Gospel hope when life doesn't make sense / Paul David Tripp.
Description: Wheaton : Crossway, 2018. | Includes bibliographical references and index.
Identifiers: LCCN 2018032547 (print) | LCCN 2018033071 (ebook) | ISBN 9781433556784 (pdf) |
    ISBN 9781433556791 (mobi) | ISBN 9781433556807 (epub) | ISBN 9781433556777 (hc)
Subjects: LCSH: Suffering—Religious aspects—Christianity.
Classification: LCC BV4909 (ebook) | LCC BV4909 .T75 2018 (print) | DDC 248.8/6—dc23
LC record available at https://lccn.loc.gov/2018032547

Crossway is a publishing ministry of Good News Publishers.

LB		28	27	26	25	24	23	22	21	20	19	18
15	14	13	12	11	10	9	8	7	6	5	4	3	2	1

To all those who have walked suffering's
rocky and twisting pathway,
this book is for you.

Contents

Introduction

It was a surprise visit by an unwelcome visitor, like it is for so many sufferers. I didn't know that day that Mr. Hardship would knock on my door, barge his way in, and take residence in the most intimate rooms of my life. And I didn't have any idea how his presence would fundamentally change so many thing for the long run. I watched him go room to room through my life rearranging everything, wondering what things would be like if and when he finally left. If I could have, I would have evicted this unwanted stranger, but I failed at all my attempts to boot him out the door or deny that he had taken residence in my life. I spent way too much time trying to figure out why he had knocked on my door and why he had chosen this particular moment, but I never got clear answers to my questions.

Once I realized that I couldn't kick Mr. Hardship out of my life, I gave myself to trying to understand how to live with him or around him. His presence made me feel like an actor in a drama where everyone had a script but me. I felt unprepared and unable, not just the day he first entered, but day after day. Sure, I had known that Mr. Hardship was out there, and I had heard the stories of how he had entered other people's doors, but somehow I didn't think it would happen to me. Embarrassment washed over me as I thought of the silly platitudes and empty answers I had casually given people when they'd been caught in the confusing drama I was now in. And I thought about how foolish I'd been to think that this unwanted stranger who, somehow, someway, enters everyone's door, would for some reason omit mine.

Because I did not have the power or control to make Mr. Hardship leave, I ran to the place where I have always found wisdom, hope, and rest of heart. I ran to the gospel of Jesus Christ, and in so doing, into the arms of my Savior. As I dove into the narrative of the gospel, which is the core message of God's Word, I realized something profoundly important and wonderfully comforting: I wasn't unprepared after all. The message of God's sovereign control over me and my world, the gospel's honesty about life in this fallen world, the comfort of the right-here, right-now presence and grace of the Savior, and the insight into the spiritual war that rages in my heart had prepared me well for the entrance and presence of this unwelcome stranger.

I am no longer angry or discouraged that Mr. Hardship entered my door unexpectedly that day. Although I still struggle with the pain and weakness that he has left me with, I know that I am better off because of his presence. No, I don't like the travail of pain or loss anymore than you do, but in my suffering, a miraculous thing happened: Mr. Hardship became a tool of my Savior to produce very good things in me, things that I am sure could not have been produced any other way.

Sure, there are times I get tired and wish he'd up and leave, but I don't get despondent. I know I haven't been ignored or forsaken, because long before Mr. Hardship entered my door, my Savior had taken permanent residence in my life. This means through all of this drama, I have not been left alone to deal with Mr. Hardship on my own. My Savior has been with me, for me, and in me, and he works to take very bad things and produce through them very, very good things. He has done that for me, and he will continue to do that.

So I write this book for those who also have been suddenly invaded by the same unwanted stranger. I write so that you too would feel loved, prepared, and thankful, no, not for the pain, but for the One who is there with you in your pain. He is the One who not only comforts you but produces beautiful things in you and through you out of what you didn't invite into your life and don't really want in your life and out of what doesn't seem good at all.

1

The Day My Life Changed

October 19, 2014, is a day I will never forget, because it's the day my life changed. I didn't want my life to change, hadn't planned for my life to change, but my life changed. It was unexpected and unwanted, out of the blue and out of my control. I didn't see it coming. Sometimes big changes come with warnings. Sometimes you can see the dark clouds on the horizon. Sometimes it's a weird feeling or an anxious thought that alerts you to something around the corner. But I was totally surprised and completely unprepared for what was about to be put on my plate.

I was away on a ministry trip and began to have some minor symptoms, but they were sufficiently minimal that I had no hint of what was about to come. But because I am no longer a recent graduate from college and am at the age when it's important to pay attention to messages your body gives you, I immediately called my physician when I got home. He suggested that because I live in Center City, Philadelphia, just a couple blocks from a huge hospital, that I go there and have them check me out. He assured me that it didn't sound like something to be fearful about and that they'd probably examine me and send me home.

The next day was Sunday, so the plan was that Luella, my wife, and I would go to church, get something to eat afterward, and then walk over to the hospital. We were so relaxed about the whole thing that we stopped at a neighborhood Starbucks on the way. We checked into the emergency room at Jefferson Hospital, knowing we would be in for a long wait, and settled in to watch the Philadelphia Eagles. I sat there more impatient to be seen by a doctor than anxious about what I would be told. Finally I was called back and asked to describe my symptoms, while my vitals were being taken.

It wasn't long before there were four physicians from different departments in the little emergency room. I asked what was going on but never got a direct answer. To my left I heard two of the doctors discussing dialysis. It made no sense to me; I thought, *What in the world are they talking about?* It didn't seem possible that I was that sick. I didn't feel sick. I had done my regular daily ten-mile bike sprint that week. I had just spoken for six hours over the weekend with all the energy I always have. I thought they must have the wrong chart, that they must be looking at the wrong symptoms. But those doctors weren't in the wrong examining room. In a flash, painful procedures were being done on me, and before long, I was admitted for what would become a ten-day stay. It was confusing and disconcerting, to say the least. I didn't understand what was going on; all I knew for sure was that a leisurely afternoon had suddenly become very serious and very painful. But I had no preparation for what was about to happen next.

Almost immediately after arriving in my hospital room, I went into a full-body spasm. I will never be able to adequately describe it to you. This was pain like I never knew existed, and during the spasms the pain was focused on my groin area, where it felt as if someone had stuck me with a knife. The spasms came with ferocity every two or three minutes, and when they came,

I screamed. When you're scared, you sometimes scream for help because you hope someone will hear and come to the rescue. These were not that type of scream. The pain was so intolerable that involuntary screams just came out of me. And in between my screams I cried in despair, "God, help me! God, help me!" It was terrifying to go through. I was not afraid of the next day; I was terrified of the next five minutes and the torture the spasms would bring.

I screamed for thirty-six hours, and as I screamed, I couldn't understand why someone in the hospital didn't help me. I couldn't grasp why they didn't do something to relieve my pain. One nurse told me not to let my body tense up when the spasms came because that made them worse. She might as well have told me to jump over the moon. When the spasms came, I lost all ability to control my physical responses. After a particularly horrible and longer-than-usual spasm, in tears I looked at Luella and told her I wanted to die. I just wanted the torture to stop, and it seemed impossible that someone couldn't do something to help me with my pain.

Compounding my pain was confusion. I had no idea what was happening to me. I had no idea how I had gotten from a relaxing chai with Luella at Starbucks that afternoon to this horrid scene. I had no concept of what was happening in my body that would somehow make sense of all this. And I had no idea what the doctors were doing behind the scenes to deal with whatever was going on inside me. The suddenness and irrationality of it all just made what I was experiencing all the more difficult. I wanted it all to stop, and I didn't care how.

In one of those moments when I was crying out, wondering why no one was doing anything to relieve my pain, my son Ethan said, "Dad, they're not worried about your pain right now; they're worried about saving your life. When you're stable, they'll give you something for your pain." Those words were enormously helpful. And there did come a moment when they gave me something to lessen the pain of those spasms.

What I'd thought would be a checkup became a ten-day hospital stay. And for the first few days I didn't know what I was dealing with. I knew something was terribly wrong, and so Steve, who manages my ministry life, began canceling upcoming ministry events. I lay in bed, exhausted and discouraged and in constant discomfort. They had inserted a catheter, and I bled into the catheter for the entire ten days, sometimes painfully passing rather large blood clots.

How had I gotten so sick so quickly? What was wrong, and how would it be fixed? Was I in the right medical hands? How long would I be in the hospital? How would all of this alter my life? What impact would it have in my ministry? What would it mean for Luella and my children? What in the world was God doing? These were some of the questions that rattled around in my brain as I lay in that bed bleeding into a bag.

About the third day in, the kidney doctor who had been assigned to my case came in and informed me that my kidneys had been significantly damaged. I would learn later that when I arrived at the hospital, I was in acute kidney failure. If I had waited seven to ten more days, my kidneys would have died, and I would not be writing this book. It was shocking and unreal to hear. I had walked into the hospital with the identity of a healthy man. I had done my fitness routine that week. I had not felt sick. But I was a very sick man with a very serious diagnosis that would forever change my life.

In ways that I had never experienced before, I felt vulnerable and small. I was haunted by the thought that there might be other things going on in my body that I didn't know about. I hadn't thought about death until now, but that thought was now with me all the time. I had never thought about living long term with illness or the effects of major damage to a very impor-

tant system in my body. I wondered if I would be able to continue
to do what God had called for me to do, and, if I couldn't, what
would we do, how would we live? I cried out for God's help, with
those exact words, because I was too shocked and confused to
know what to pray for. I grabbed hold of his promises. I tried to
preach to myself of his presence, but it was hard. In the middle of
the night it was hard when the nurse came in to change my bag,
as I lay awake in the darkness to control my thoughts. Luella
slept in the chair next to me, and I would grab her hand and cry.
I didn't even know what I was crying about; the tears just came.

When they finally released me from the hospital, I was still
a very sick man. I left the hospital with a catheter and a bag
strapped to my leg. The apparatus made it uncomfortable to sit,
sleep, or walk. I wasn't used to the apparatus, so I made disgust-
ing messes. It all was mortifying and a bit dehumanizing. But
I believe that God is good, and I did everything I could to run
toward his goodness and not away from it. As I got stronger I
traveled to conferences to speak with the bag strapped to my leg
and the fear each time that I would not have the strength to get
through the entire weekend.

During the first post-hospital-release appointment with my
physician, I was told of the severity of my kidney damage and
directed to the nephrologist who would handle my follow-up
care. When I saw my kidney doctor I was told that I had lost
65 percent of my kidney function and that the damage could
not be reversed. I left that appointment weighed down by the
long list of life-changing effects from the kidney damage. Little
did I know that I was not at the end of my physical travail, but
at the beginning.

Soon after, I was informed that I needed a rather major surgery. Coming just a few months after I'd been released from
the hospital, it was a blow. I had just begun to climb my way
back physically and into my ministry life, and I was about to be

physically knocked down again and have my ministry life inter-rupted again. You cannot go through things like this without wondering what God is doing and without at least being tempted to doubt his wisdom, goodness, and love. I did face those temp-tations, but I would not let my heart go there. I held onto God's promises even in the middle of the disappointment and confu-sion. But it was very discouraging. I did grapple with the seeming irrationality of it all; how did it make sense that at the moment of my greatest ministry influence, I would be rendered weaker than I had ever been?

After surgery, I once again thought that I was on the road to the recovery of my normal life, but recovery was not the plan. About three months after my surgery and second hospital stay, I was informed that I would need another surgery. Scar tissue had developed that put my kidneys at risk, and since I didn't have much kidney left, surgery was essential. The day of my second surgery I was awakened at about four-thirty in the morning to head to the hospital to get prepped. I was anxious about the surgery but discouraged with the prospects of its effects. I knew I would be knocked back physically and have to start the re-covery process all over again. I knew that my life and ministry would be put on hold again. And I knew that I had no power whatsoever to keep all that from happening.

Physical suffering exposes the delusion of personal autonomy and self-sufficiency. If you and I had the kind of control that we fall into thinking we have, none of us would ever go through anything difficult. None of us would choose to be sick. None of us would choose to experience physical pain. None of us likes the prospect of being physically weak and disabled. None of us likes our lives being put on hold. Physical suffering does force you to face the reality that your life is in the hands of another. It reminds you that you are small and dependent, that whatever little bits of power and control you have can be taken away in an instant. Independence is a delusion that is quickly exposed by suffering.

I found what I was going through to be not only discouraging in many ways but also deeply humbling. My weakness enabled me to see and admit to things that I had never faced in myself before. My sickness redefined who I thought I was and what I thought of my walk with God. Let me explain. During these months I was confronted with the reality that much of what I thought was faith in Christ was actually confidence in my physical condition and pride in my ability to produce. I had always had lots of energy and was quite physically fit for my age. I never remember being very tired, never required much sleep, and was always able to be productive. I used to proudly say that sleep was a necessary interruption to an otherwise productive day. Suffering has the power to expose what you have been trusting all along. If you lose your hope when your physical body fails, maybe your hope wasn't really in your Savior after all. It was humbling to confess that what I thought was faith was actually self-reliance.

But God wasn't done with me yet. Contrary to what I expected and would have planned, I wasn't done with surgery or the hospital stays and the suspended life that would follow. Almost four months later, with a body that had not yet fully recovered, I found myself being wheeled into surgery again. More scar tissue had developed, creating more blockages and putting my kidneys at risk once again. Each surgery was followed by catheterization and that bag attached to my leg. Each surgery resulted in lots of pain, profound weakness, and sleepless nights. Each surgery was accompanied by the spiritual battle of heart and mind. Each surgery was followed by all the temptations that greet everyone who suffers in this broken world. Each time, I was reminded that suffering is spiritual warfare.

The best way to characterize my discouragement at that time is by something that I tearfully said to Luella more than once: "All I want is Paul back again!" The old Paul is what I longed for, the one with endless energy and a body that functions without medical assistance. I wanted the old Paul who could deal with a ridiculously busy schedule and never feel stressed or tired. I hated being sick, weak, and tired, and I hated the fact that I couldn't free myself from the cycle of surgeries I was trapped in. I didn't hate God, I didn't jettison my theology, and I didn't bring God into the court of my judgment to question his wisdom and love, but I did struggle to accept what had been put on my plate. I didn't look good, I didn't feel good, and I had little energy to do the things that God had called me to do. I intended to spend some hours writing, but many of those days I got up with so little energy of body and mind that all I could do was sit in a chair.

I got through the day by taking naps, something I had never done before. I used to make fun of people who couldn't cope without their daily nap. I now looked forward to my nap. It was all very disorienting and disheartening. I didn't recognize the person I had become and couldn't relate to the level of inability I felt. As all this was washing over me, I got more bad news: I would need yet another surgery. I will shorten the story here. I kept needing surgery after surgery until I had sustained six surgeries in two years! Never did my body have enough time to recover. Weakness built upon weakness, symptoms piled upon symptoms, and the war within raged. No one's body can tolerate surgery after surgery in the same anatomical area. I did wonder if in the attempt to save my kidneys, other parts of my body were being irreparably damaged.

My sixth surgery was the biggest and most difficult yet. My surgeon had avoided doing this surgery because it was so invasive and painful and would be followed by a lengthy and difficult recovery period. But it was clear that it needed to be done. It was very difficult and painful and left me essentially homebound for two months.

I still don't know what I am facing physically. It has been six months since that last big surgery, and my symptoms are as manageable as possible at this point, but I have been left a physically damaged man. I will never again be able to do ministry the way I had done it for years. I will never again have the energy I once had. I will always be limited by the results of major damage to an essential organ. And since my ministry was largely funded by weekend conferences, my physical suffering has brought with it financial stresses for me and my ministry team. We've had to make hard decisions, decisions none of us wanted to make. We've had to ask hard questions that we never thought we would need to ask. We've had to confess our dependency on God in deeper ways than we have ever confessed it before. And we've had to thank God for a new normal that we would have never chosen for ourselves.

Why Start This Book with My Story?

Suffering is never abstract, theoretical, or impersonal. Suffering is real, tangible, personal, and specific. The Bible never presents suffering as an idea or a concept but puts it before us in the blood-and-guts drama of real human experiences. When it comes to suffering, Scripture is never avoidant or cosmetic in its approach. The Bible never minimizes the harsh experiences of life in this terribly broken world, and in so doing, the Bible forces us out of our denial and toward humble honesty. In fact, the Bible is so honest about suffering that it recounts stories that are so weird and dark that if they were a Netflix video you probably wouldn't watch it.

Scripture never looks down on the sufferer, it never mocks his pain, it never turns a deaf ear to his cries, and it never condemns him for his struggle. It presents to the sufferer a God who understands, who cares, who invites us to come to him for help, and who promises one day to end all suffering of any kind once and forever. Because of this, the Bible, while being dramatically honest about suffering, is at the same time gloriously hopeful. And it's not just that the Bible tells the story of suffering honestly and authentically; it also gives us concrete and real hope.

I had no interest in writing a book that essentially laid out a theoretical theology of suffering, because I think that would have been an unbiblical handling of what the Bible has to say about suffering. The entire discussion of suffering is done at street level where the mud and blood of suffering splashes up and in some way stains us all. This is why I have told you my story, a story that I am still living out every day. Last week I went without one night of real sleep. The weakness washed over me, and I was reminded that my travail is not over because some systems in my body are irreparably broken. I want this book to live where sufferers live, to speak to sufferers' cries, and to practically address the things that every sufferer grapples with.

So this book will place the gorgeous, honest, and hopeful theology of suffering, which is a core theme of the redemptive story, into the context of an actual sufferer's story. Beautiful truths will be presented and understood in connection with real human pain and struggle. Remember that the theology of suffering in Scripture is never, ever an end in itself but is designed as a means to the end of real comfort, real direction, real protection, real conviction, and real hope. This concrete way of dealing with what Scripture teaches forces us away from platitudes and denial and toward concrete understanding and candor.

If you are suffering now, I invite you to take this journey with me; my hope is that I will give words to your struggle and rest in the midst of your pain. If you are not suffering now, look around, because someone near you is, and this book will put you inside their experience and help you know what it's like to love them, to walk with them, and to help them bear that burden. And if you are not suffering now, you will someday. Somehow, someway, suffering enters everyone's door. Sometimes you see it coming, and other times it blindsides you, but it will come because we are imperfect people who inflict suffering on one another, and we all are unable to completely escape the brokenness of the world that is our present address.

Because of the amazing practical wisdom of God's Word, the glory of God's presence and power, and the reality of mercies that are new every morning, we do not have to run from this topic. We can stare it in the face with open and expectant hearts. Remember that the hope of redemption is not just reserved for eternity but is a real, living, present hope. This hope is rooted in the fact that your Lord is in you, he is with you, and he is for you right here, right now. And this truth radically changes how we understand, experience, and respond to the suffering that has or surely will come our way. So with gospel courage read on, knowing that there is no valley of suffering so deep that God's grace in Jesus isn't deeper.

Review and Reflect

1. How do you see the Lord's providence in Paul Tripp's health crisis?

2. Paul speaks of clinging to God's promises and crying out for his help. How does having an understanding and belief in God help in times of suffering?

3. Paul Tripp states that "Scripture never looks down on the sufferer" (p. 23). How does that encourage you?

4. Have you ever considered that at its core, suffering is spiritual warfare?

5. When you pray that your hope would be "rooted in the fact that your Lord is in you, he is with you, and he is for you right here, right now" (p. 25), how can you look differently at suffering?

Heart Reset

- Psalm 13:1–6; 27:1–14

- Isaiah 43:1

2

Suffering Is Never Neutral

I wish I could say that my experience of suffering was neutral, but it wasn't, and it isn't for anybody else either. Here's what every sufferer needs to understand: *you never just suffer the thing that you're suffering, but you always also suffer the way that you're suffering that thing.* You and I never come to our suffering empty-handed. We always drag a bag full of experiences, expectations, assumptions, perspectives, desires, intentions, and decisions into our suffering. So our lives are shaped not just by what we suffer but by what we bring to our suffering. What you think about yourself, life, God, and others will profoundly affect the way you think about, interact with, and respond to the difficulty that comes your way.

This is humbling to admit, but there were two things I didn't know I was carrying into my physical travail that shaped how I walked my way through the experience. First was *pride*. I was unaware that there was a lot of pride in me—pride in physical health and in accomplishment. About three years before I got sick, I lost 40 pounds, changed my whole relationship to food, and began to exercise more aggressively. It worked. I kept the weight off and felt younger and more energetic than I had for years. I was proud of my physical fitness and confident in the healthiness of my body. I was proud too that because I was physically strong, I was able to be productive. I traveled every weekend to conferences around the world and wrote book after book in between. I look back and now see that I lived with assessments of invincibility. I was not a young man, but I felt like I was at the top of my game. Health and success are intoxicating but also vulnerable.

When I realized I was very ill and that weakness and fatigue would be with me for the rest of my life, the blow was not just physical, but emotional and spiritual as well. Honestly, I didn't suffer just physical pain, but also the even more profound pain of the death of my delusion of invincibility and the pride of productivity. These are subtle but deeply ingrained identity issues. I would've told you that my identity was firmly rooted in Christ, and there are significant ways in which it was, but underneath were artifacts of self-reliance.

Now, here's what happens in times of suffering. When the thing you have been trusting (whether you knew it or not) is laid to waste, you don't suffer just the loss of that thing; you also suffer the loss of the identity and security that it provided. This may not make sense to you if right now you are going through something that you wouldn't have planned for yourself, but the weakness that is now a part of my regular life has been a huge instrument of God's grace (see 2 Cor. 12:9.) It has done two things for me. First, it has exposed an *idol of self* I did not know was there. Pride in my physical heath and my ability to produce made me take credit for what I couldn't have produced on my own. God created and controls my physical body, and God has given me the gifts that I employ every day. Physical health and productivity should produce deeper gratitude and worship, not self-reliance and pride in productivity. I am thankful for what my weakness has exposed and for being freed by grace from having to prove any longer that I am what I think I am.

But there's a second thing that has been wonderful to understand. Perhaps we curse physical weakness because we are uncomfortable with placing our trust in God. Let me explain. Weakness simply demonstrates what has been true all along: we are completely dependent on God for life and breath and everything else. Weakness was not the end for me, but a new beginning, because weakness provides the context in which true strength is found. Paul says in 2 Corinthians 12:9 that he'll boast in his weakness. It sounds weird and crazy when you first read it, but it's not. He has come to know that God's "power is made perfect" in his weakness. You see, weakness is not what you and I should be afraid of. We should fear our delusion of strength. Strong people tend not to reach out for help, because they think they don't need it. When you have been proven weak, you tap into the endless resources of divine power that are yours in Christ. In my weakness I have known strength that I never knew before.

The second thing that shaped the way I suffered physically was *unrealistic expectations*. Suffering shouldn't surprise us, but it almost always does, and it surely surprised me. Now, this is humbling to admit because I wrote a book about living with the reality of the fall in view.[1] I did go into my sickness with my theology in the right place. I did believe that I lived in a groaning world crying out for redemption, but it was battling with something else inside me. There was this expectation that I would always be as I had been, that is, that I would always be strong and healthy. There was little room in my life, family, and ministry plans for weakness within or trouble without. In fact, there was no room for any disruption at all. So much of the way

---

1. Paul David Tripp, *Broken-Down House: Living Productively in a World Gone Bad* (Wapwallopen, PA: Shepherd Press, 2009).

I thought about myself and planned was based on the unrealistic expectation that I would continue to escape the regular disruption of one's life and plans that happens in a world that doesn't operate as God designed it to operate.

I wasn't singled out; God hadn't forgotten me or turned his back. I wasn't being punished for my choices, and I wasn't receiving the expected consequences for poor decisions. My story is about the regular things that happen to us all because we live in a world that has been dramatically damaged by sin. In this world sickness and disease live, and our bodies break down or don't function properly. In this world pain, sometimes chronic and sometimes acute, assaults us and makes life nearly unlivable. We live in a broken world where people die, food decays, wars rage, governments are corrupt, people take what isn't theirs and inflict violence on one another, spouses act hatefully toward each another, children are abused instead of protected, people slowly die of starvation or die suddenly from disease, sexual and gender confusion lives, drugs addict and destroy, gossip destroys reputations, lust and greed control hearts, bitterness grows like a cancer, and the list could go on and on.

The Bible doesn't pull any punches. At every turn, it informs and warns us about the nature of the world, which is the address where we all live. Whether it's a dramatic narrative of life, or a doctrine that informs, or a wisdom principle about how to live well, Scripture works to prepare us, not so we would live in fear, but so we will be ready for the things we will all face. God gives us everything we need so that we will live with realistic expectations and so that moments of difficulty will not be full of shock, fear, and panic, but experienced with faith, calm, and confident choices.

Although I had right theology in place, somehow, at street level, my expectations were unrealistic, and unrealistic expectations always make suffering harder. My point is that I am a living example of the truth that you and I never suffer just the thing that we're suffering, but we also suffer the way that we're suffering it. Each of us brings to our suffering things that shape the way that we suffer. We all suffer, but we don't suffer the same way, because our suffering is shaped by what we carry into the difficulties that come our way.

Here's what is so important to understand, and what may be the principal contribution of this book: your suffering is more powerfully shaped by what's in your heart than by what's in your body or in the world around you. Now, don't misunderstand what I am saying. My suffering was real, the dysfunction in my body was real, the damage to my kidneys is real, the pain I went through was horribly real, and the weakness that is now my normal life is real. But the way that I experienced all those harsh realities was shaped by the thoughts, desires, dreams, expectations, cravings, fears, and assumptions of my heart. The same is true for you. Your responses to the situations in your life, whether physical, relational, or circumstantial, are always more determined by what is inside you (your heart) than by the things you are facing. This is why people have dramatically different responses to the same situations of difficulty. This is why the writer of Proverbs says:

Keep your heart with all vigilance,
    for from it flow the springs of life. (Prov. 4:23)

Like a stream, your attitudes, choices, reactions, decisions, and responses to whatever you are facing flow out of your heart. The heart is the center of your personhood. The heart is your causal core, as dry soil soaks in the liquid of a stream. Suffering draws out the true thoughts, attitudes, assumptions, and desires of your heart. So it's helpful to consider the kinds of things we bring to our suffering that cause us to trouble our own trouble.

What Do You Bring to Your Suffering?

Case study!

Following is a suggestive, not exhaustive, list of the kinds of things that we bring to moments of suffering that deepen the pain of the painful thing we are facing.

1. Poor Theology

Remember that every human being thinks and lives theologically. Whether you're aware of it or not, you carry around a well-developed personal worldview that shapes the way you interpret and deal with everything that comes your way. That worldview gives some kind of answer to questions like: Who is God? What is he doing? Why is he doing what he's doing? Who am I? What is the reason for my life? What does it look like to live a successful life? What is right and wrong? Why do certain things happen? Where are hope, purpose, and motivation to be found? Again, this is not an exhaustive list but representative of the kinds of questions that everybody asks and somehow answers.

Since your thoughts always precede and determine your actions, the theology you carry into times of suffering and trial are very, very important. Let me give you two examples of how bad theology worsens your experience of suffering. The first goes like this: *I am suffering because God is punishing me for my sin.*

Sue had to deal not only with a very serious disease that had invaded her body, but also with paralyzing guilt and shame. Why, you may ask? Because Sue was convinced that her disease was God's punishment for bad choices and decisions she had made. In a time when she needed to run to God, she did her best to hide from him and to hide from his people. She reasoned that her job was to endure the punishment she deserved.

Clearly, thinking like Sue's is rooted in very bad theology. The message of Scripture is that every piece of the guilt, shame, and punishment for our sin was completely and once for all carried by Christ. This means there is no more condemnation for those in Christ Jesus (see Rom. 8:1–4). So our suffering is not punitive, that is, not a direct punishment for sins we have committed.

How discouraging not only to go through hard and maybe even life-altering circumstances but also to think you are going through those things because you've fallen short of God's standard. It's hard to run to God for help, to rest in his care, to be assured of his love, and to believe that his mercies are constantly available and new every day when you're convinced you're being punished by him. And it's hard to reach out for God's grace when you think he's giving you what you deserve. The Bible never interprets our suffering this way; in fact, it teaches the opposite. Rather than suffering being connected to the bad things we have done, Scripture connects trials and difficulty to the good things God wants for us and is working to produce in us (see James 1:2–4).

The second example flows out of a poor understanding of Romans 8:28, which says, "We know that for those who love God all things work together for good, for those who are called according to his purpose." Sadly, this verse has been interpreted by many to promise that everything you go through will turn out all right in the end. This interpretation leads people to harbor unrealistic expectations of a happy ending to something they are suffering, and in so doing, causes them to think that God has failed to deliver what he has promised when suffering continues or leaves them with lives that are forever altered.

Jim was sure, because of what he had been taught that Romans 8:28 promised, that what he had lost would surely be returned. Because of the fraud of someone he trusted, Jim had lost everything he'd worked for. He went from being a wealthy executive to an hourly laborer, and during the first few years he was motivated by the thought that it would all turn out for the best. But as year lapped upon year, Jim got more discouraged and angry. He drifted away from his small group and eventually quit going to church altogether. Bitterness with God came from wrongly understood expectations, and those expectations in the end had a much greater impact on Jim's life than the terrible loss he'd suffered.

When people lift Romans 8:28 out of its immediate context, they understand it to mean what it does not mean. The way to understand any single Bible passage is to remember that Scripture interprets Scripture. The key to understanding the true hope of this passage is to understand the "good" that Paul is writing about. Verses 29 and 30 tell us. The "good" that is guaranteed in this passage is our redemption. Even before he made the world, God made the decision that his work in us would be completed no matter what. This means that the grace you and I reach out for in our times of trouble is never shaky or at risk; it is a present expression of a plan that was settled before this world began. It is so good to know that when things in you and around you have been damaged or compromised, nothing can damage, interrupt, or stop your true security, which is found in God and his grace poured out for you. This proper understanding of this wonderful passage gives hope even when you look around and have no hope.

I have given you just two examples of the powerful influence that poor theology will have on the way you suffer through what is already hard on its own. Sue and Jim not only were suffering but were victims of the bad theology that they brought to that difficulty.

2. Doubt of God

Suffering doesn't so much change your heart as expose what has been in your heart all along. Difficulty has an amazing ability to reveal what's inside us. Trials reveal your true thoughts and desires, where you have been looking for life, where you have sought meaning, and where you have looked to give you hope. Suffering will always expose the true nature of your relationship to and communion with God. I won't say much here, because a later chapter is dedicated to this topic, but your suffering will be all the more painful if you question the presence, promises, goodness, or faithfulness of God.

3. Unrealistic Expectations of Life

I wrote in this first chapter of my unrealistic expectations, but I want to put this topic of unrealistic expectations into two categories that I think linger unrecognized and unaddressed by many. First is the expectation that what is will always be. In Romans 8:21 we read that the world we now live in is in "bondage to corruption." Paul means that decay is an ever-present reality. Nothing remains the same. Bodies grow old, friendships sour, marriages grow distant, churches fall into difficulty, government lurches into corruption. Somehow, someway, all the good things around us are under constant attack. Change is a constant reality. But we all tend to get lulled into thinking that what we have today will be with us tomorrow and the tomorrows that follow.

The second thing concerning expectations is that we tend not to take seriously the dramatic brokenness of the world we live in. Romans 8:22 tells us that we live in a "groaning" world. You groan when you feel weak. You groan when you are in pain. You groan when something has been damaged. You groan when you are discouraged. You groan when you wonder if what has caused you to groan will ever end. You groan when you can't find words to express your cries. If you don't take seriously the groaning condition of our world, you will live with naive expectations of what your life will be, you will be unprepared for the trouble that comes your way, and you will be susceptible to the myriad of temptations that come your way.

4. Unrealistic Expectations of Others

We do forget that everyone around us is a sinner, that no one has consistently correct thoughts, completely pure desires, or regularly pure motives. Even if you're surrounded by believers, it's important to remember that although the dominating power of sin has been broken in them, the presence of sin still remains, even though it is being progressively rooted out by God's grace. That means we are all sinned against, and we all sin against others. All of us deal with relational misunderstanding, conflict, hurt, misjudgment, and rejection.

It never works to turn a person into your personal messiah. It never works to look to another for your identity. It never works to ask people to give you meaning and purpose. It is unrealistic to look to someone for inner peace. It never goes well when you ask another flawed human being to be the source of your happiness. There is an ever-faithful Messiah, and no one around you is capable of taking his place and doing for you what he alone can do.

Suffering is intensified when we elevate people too high in our hearts and then they fail us.

5. Pride

By pride here, I mean not the pride of arrogance but rather the pride of self-reliance. There are many people who, like me, mistake self-confidence for faith in Christ. We're proud of our physical strength and health, our sharp minds, our social abilities, our ability to lead and control, and our successes. In this way we tend to take credit for things we could never produce or achieve on our own. We forget that every cell in our body and every neuron in our brain is dependent on God. We forget that every success we've achieved has depended on forces we could never control, and we forget that all our natural abilities are gifts from God.

Taking too much credit always leads to placing too much trust in yourself.

When you live self-reliantly, and the unexpected, the unplanned, the unwanted, or the painful comes your way, you panic. You panic because suddenly you're faced with your smallness, weakness, and vulnerability. You panic because you feel unprepared and unable. You panic because things are out of your control. You panic because you can't understand or make sense of what is going on. You panic because the way out is unclear. You panic because you just don't know what to do.

Suffering exposes the danger of self-reliance. It reminds us that we were not designed to live independently but in dependence on God and others. This is true not just because sin has entered the world; it was true of Adam and Eve in a perfect world, because it's how God designed people to live.

6. Materialism

This word begs definition. By *materialism*, I don't mean that you're chasing after the idol of material things, that you're always craving the next physical thing. I'm thinking here of our tendency to place too much of our security and hope in physical things, in our house and possessions or the health of our body or in our job, bank account, or retirement plan.

Every human being looks to something for security. When you've looked to physical things for your security, and those things fail you or are taken away, you lose that fundamental sense of well-being that everyone longs for. I can't tell you how many people I've counseled who lost themselves when they lost their job.

The only safe place to look for a sturdy well-being of heart is the Creator. The material things God created can never do for you what only God can do. When you've been asking material things to give you what they were never meant to give, the loss of those things will be an even more crushing blow than the physical loss.

7. Selfism

As I've said and written before, the DNA of sin is selfishness (see 2 Cor. 5:15). Sin causes us to stick ourselves in the center of our world and make life all about us. It causes us to reduce the field of our daily concerns to the small agenda of our wants, our needs, and our feelings. Sin causes us to be driven by selfish desires, a spirit of entitlement, and a silent list of demands. Sin causes us to want our own way, to want sovereignty over things we weren't designed to control, and to want to coerce others into the service of our agenda. None of us, this side of eternity, is able to completely escape the self-ism of sin. This heart tendency toward functional me-ism always makes suffering more difficult.

Suffering confronts us with the fact that life is not about us but about God. It is not about our glory but his. It's not first about our pleasure but about his. It's not about our plans for us but about his will for us. It's not about our control but his. It's not about our little kingdoms but about his. It's not about our successes but about the display of his majesty.

If life were about us and controlled by us, we would see to it that we never suffer. The crisis of faith that often accompanies suffering is the result of a collision between our will and God's will and our glory and his glory. In our selfishness we can't see suffering of any kind as good, so we begin to question whether God, who has allowed it into our lives, is good. Putting yourself in the center will make the trouble you face all the more troublesome.

Sarah was facing very hard things. She had been plotted against and abandoned by her husband, she had lost custody of her children, and she had been left financially destitute. What had been done to her was horribly wrong, but her emotional and spiritual devastation was the result not only of the terrible wrongs that had been done to her but also of critical beliefs that she had carried into those wrongs. Sarah was a believer, but at street level, God was neither the source of her security nor her hope. She had married into wealth and luxury; she had a beautiful house and a great circle of friends. It was the good life, not the gospel, that got her up every morning. It was all the things around her and all the things she experienced that made her happy. The gospel of Jesus Christ was her theology but didn't provide security for her heart or drive the way that she lived. She understood that she had been forgiven by grace and would spend an eternity with the Lord, but there was a huge gap in the middle of her grasp of the gospel. So her life became her personal messiah, giving her what it was never meant to give.

When Henry walked out never to return and took literally everything with him, Sarah didn't lose just Henry, the house, and the kids—she lost herself. As I listened to Sarah talk, I realized that what made this horrible sin against her even more devastating was that in losing all these things, Sarah lost her functional savior, and in losing her functional savior, she lost her will to go on. And it was when Sarah got hold of this truth that her heart began to lift, her hope began to return, and she decided to live again.

It really is true that we never come empty-handed to any experience. And we surely always drag something into the suffering that enters our door. What about you? What are you carrying around that has the power to cause you to trouble your own trouble? What has the power to allow you to forget that no matter what painful thing you're enduring, as God's child it's impossible for you to endure it all by yourself? The One who created this world and rules it with wisdom, righteousness, and love is in you, with you, and for you, and nothing has the power to separate you from his love.

Review and Reflect

1. How are trust and identity connected? What have you put your trust in other than God?

2. Paul Tripp writes, "We should fear our delusion of strength" (p. 29). Considering the chapter as a whole, what does this mean?

3. "Scripture works to prepare us, not so we would live in fear, but so we will be ready for the things we will all face" (p. 30). Identify some passages or biblical stories to cling to in moments of suffering.

4. Have you questioned God regarding your suffering because you've thought it was punishment? What Scripture verses refute this belief?

5. Consider the things that can be brought to your suffering (poor theology, doubt of God, unrealistic expectations of life and of others, pride, materialism, and selfism). Pray that the Lord would expose your weakness and dependency and show you his care.

Heart Reset

- Romans 8:1–4

- 2 Corinthians 12:9

- James 1:2–4

3

The Awareness Trap

Suffering is real. Pain is real. Cries for relief are normal. This is what was in Shirley's mind all the time. She wondered if people really understood how real it all was. The car that hit Shirley as she crossed the street on the summer shopping jaunt was real. The injuries she sustained were real, and their crippling effects on her daily life were both real and inescapable. Her chronic pain was not an idea; it was a real trauma that greeted her every morning and followed her throughout her day. It made sleeping difficult and staying awake arduous.

When Shirley shared her travail with others, she walked away thinking they heard just words, concepts without much reality. She felt again and again that well-meaning people thought they could "fix" her with words. She had heard every Christian and not-so-Christian cliché. She did not know what to do with the fact that what was very real to her seemed unreal to the people around her.

There are thousands and thousands of Shirleys. Perhaps you're one of them. You are very aware of the fact that what is normal to you is way outside of what is normal for the people around you, that what are daily realities for you are just concepts to them, and what they say to you never has the power to take away the one thing you'd like to be rid of—your pain. You know they don't mean it, but it seems that they always end up minimizing the gravity of your experience. They want to help, they think they've helped, but they haven't. And you are frustrated that you cannot put your travail into words that they would once and for all understand. The distance between their understanding and your reality is one of the painful additions to what you are already suffering.

Here's my experience. When people ask me how I'm doing, I don't know how to answer. When I say I'm better, they hear me say that I'm okay when I'm actually not okay. I will forever live with the implications and results of the kidney damage I have sustained. If someone with knowledge of my medical problems asks me if I'm facing another surgery, and I say no, they think that my physical issues have been dealt with, and I've moved on. It's hard to know what to communicate that will give people a sense of what I continue to deal with without sounding overly dramatic. I *am* thankful that I am not facing another surgery at this point. I *am* thankful that I feel better, but I am also very aware of the limits I will live with for the rest of my life and the fact that those around me don't really grasp the difficulty of living with those limits.

Suffering is real, and its physical, spiritual, and relational effects are real. We should all take comfort in the fact that the Bible never treats suffering as anything but a real, significant, and often life-changing human experience. The content of the Bible is again and again punctuated with stories of suffering. Scripture records the real travail of real people. Disease, rape, weakness, murder, corrupt government, racism, famine, domestic violence, injustice, war, torture, betrayal, poverty, and death are some of the things that the Bible presents as the real suffering of real people.

Not only does Scripture record the history of sufferers, but a large portion of Scripture is dedicated to giving voice to their cries. I have always thought that the psalms are in the Bible to keep us honest about the messy nature of faith in this broken world. The largest body of content in the psalms is given to lament, in which the psalmist "laments" or mourns the situation he is in and the distress he is facing. There are about sixty-seven lament psalms. That means that roughly 44 percent of the content of the psalms is given over to psalms of suffering and sorrow. Not only does the Bible not minimize our suffering, but it also gives a lot of room for the voicing of our cries. In a real way the psalms record the emotional and spiritual drama of everyone who has ever suffered.

But the Bible does even more than that—it presents to us a suffering Savior. There was no relief to the travail of Jesus. It began with the ignominious conditions of his birth, to having to immediately flee with his parents for his life, to being essentially homeless, to being despised and rejected, to facing cruel injustice while being betrayed and forsaken by those closest to him, to facing torture and crucifixion and, finally, the ultimate torture of having the Father turn his back on him. None of us would be willing to exchange our life, no matter how hard it has been, for the life of Jesus while he was here on earth. He suffered not just in one way but in every way, and he suffered not just for a period of time but for his entire life. The One to whom we cry when we cry out in pain knows our pain because suffering of some kind was his experience from the moment of his birth until his final breath.

The War beneath the Battle

The reason I've taken the time here to write about how suffering is a real experience that Scripture in no way ever minimizes is that this book is not going to focus primarily on the physical aspect of suffering but on the spiritual war beneath it. In so doing, I don't want you to think that I am minimizing your pain. My assumption is that pain, sometimes unspeakable pain, inflicts us all somehow. I want to get you to think about and finally find comfort in the fact that our experience of suffering is never just physical. The pain that stops us in our tracks, that makes us want to pull the covers over our head and not face the day, and at moments makes us wish that we could die, is never just physical.

Here is what is so important to understand: suffering is spiritual warfare. When you are suffering, it is vital to know that you aren't just fighting for the health of your body, or for a relationship, or against racism or injustice, or for your marriage, or for your reputation, or for your job. As you fight for those things, you must also battle for your heart. Suffering always puts your heart under attack. Suffering makes us all susceptible to temptations that wouldn't have had such power over us otherwise. Suffering is never just a matter of the body but is always also a matter of the heart. It's never just an assault on our situation, but also an attack on our soul. Suffering takes us to the borders of our faith. It leads us to think about things we've never thought about before and maybe even question things we thought were settled in our hearts. Too many of us, while battling the cause of our suffering, forget to battle for our hearts.

The purpose of this book is to help you with the war beneath the battle, to alert you to places where you have to fight for your own heart and to help you to see the amazing ways your Savior meets you in your battle.

Why is suffering spiritual warfare? The answer is that you are not a machine. If something dysfunctions in a machine, the machine feels no sadness, is not tempted to worry, does not question long-held beliefs, doesn't wish for the life of another machine, and has no concern for what the future holds. But you and I are not like that. We do not live mechanically or by instinct. We think, wonder, desire, feel, ponder, dream, interpret, perceive, crave, project, etc. We live out of our hearts (see Prov. 4:23; Mark 7:14–23; and Luke 6:43–45), and our hearts are an ever-flowing fountain of interactivity. You and I never leave our lives alone. We bring a rich, multifaceted inner world of thoughts, desires, and emotions to every experience. We never leave alone anything that happens to us or around us. We push everything in our lives through our conceptual, emotional, spiritual grid (CES). Whether you are conscious of it or not you bring your particular CES to everything in your life. This means that you're not just shaped by your experiences, but you give shape to those experiences as well. You and I are never just influenced by what we suffer, but our CES influences the way we suffer.

The CES that you bring to your suffering shapes the way you see and understand it, and the short- and long-term impact it has on you. This is why two people in the very same difficult situation will have dramatically different experiences of it and responses to it. John and George both lost a lot of money when the stock market crashed some years ago, but they suffered through it in very different ways. For John, physical wealth was a large source of personal security, so when he lost a huge portion of his wealth, he not only lost money; he lost his security and was crippled by anxiety and anger. George knew he had to be a good steward of the money God had provided, but he never viewed it as a source of security; it frustrated him that he had lost so much, but it had little impact on his daily living.

Permit me to repeat something that I have spoken and written about before. As people made in God's image, none of us lives life based on the raw facts of our experiences. We all live based on our particular interpretation of those facts. In this way, the central battleground of suffering is not physical, financial, situational, or relational. The impact of suffering on all those things is real, often long-term, and sometimes breathtakingly difficult.

But the physical hardship always becomes hardship of the heart. Physical suffering soon becomes a war of thoughts and desires. Suffering yanks profound questions and cravings out of us. It forces us to examine and consider things in a new way or for the first time. It makes us wonder in ways we've never wondered, to doubt what we previously assumed, to crave what we've never desired, and to think in ways we've never thought.

Suffering exposes elements of our CES that we didn't know were there. It challenges old assumptions, often replacing them with new questions. It tempts us to want answers where God has been silent, to want more from God than we have already been told. Suffering is emotionally exhausting and spiritually burdensome. It makes us vulnerable in places we thought we were strong. Suffering is never just physical, but always also becomes suffering of the heart. This deeper battle is the reason for this book.

I wish I could say that as I've suffered in ways I never thought I would, I've suffered with a heart at complete and constant peace and rest, but I can't. My heart too has been assaulted with the cries and confusion that suffering brings. Assumptions I had carried for years worsened my travail, and cravings have made the burden heavier. I have examined things that made no sense at all. I've asked questions that have no promise of an answer. I've faced temptations that I have never faced before. I haven't run from or rejected my Lord, but my suffering hasn't been just bodily; it has been a battle of my heart as well.

What most of us fail to understand is that the impact on what our heart does with what we suffer is as powerful as the thing that we are suffering. You and I are never passive sufferers, and the pain we experience is never just physical or emotional. Suffering is a deeply theological and profoundly spiritual experience. It tends to assault deeply held beliefs and strengthen long-held doubts. But there is another element that begs discussion. Like everything else in our lives, the Bible doesn't make suffering just about us. We are not isolated individuals, trying to make sense of and cope with life on our own. In fact, we are never on our own in anything. We suffer as the creatures of God. We suffer as the subjects of God's sovereign rule. We suffer as the redeemed children of God.

This means that God is inextricably connected to and intimately involved in our suffering. Like everything else we face, suffering takes place under his sovereign rule, and it happens in the middle of his redemptive plan. Now, here's the point I want to make about this: the sense you make about God's involvement or noninvolvement in your suffering, the sense you make out of his purpose for or distance from your suffering, and the conclusions you make about his care and ability to help will have a huge influence on your experience of suffering. I will say much more later about how the Bible connects God to the things we suffer, but first I want to share two stories with you.

Suffering: Traps and Comforts

John lost his wife, and he was angry. She was the woman of his dreams. He met her at a corporation picnic and was pretty quickly smitten. He couldn't believe that she would pay him the time of day, but she did. As their romance blossomed, John felt like the luckiest man on earth. She shared many of his interests and, most important of all, his faith. As he sat on the plane with Jeannie, on the way to their honeymoon location, John couldn't believe that she had married him. He couldn't grasp that they would actually spend life together. The first four years of marriage were wonderful, just the two of them enjoying what they'd each always enjoyed but were now able to enjoy together.

Five years into the marriage the first baby came, and two years later another. And although their son and daughter brought the typical chaos into their lives, what John thought was as good as it gets got even better. John's business was thriving, Jeannie was a skilled and contented mother, and their church was a place where they felt happy and well fed. On the day of their son's seventeenth birthday, Jeannie felt nauseous and weak, but she pressed on. In the days that followed, she felt even worse, and at John's insistence she made an appointment with her doctor. She could tell that her doctor was concerned, but as he sent her for tests, he told her not to worry but to wait for the results.

The tests came back, and the news was not good. Jeannie had a virulent form of cancer that was already quite advanced. John cried with her but then said, "We will fight this thing any and every way we can." And fight they did, from clinic to clinic and one experimental drug after another, but Jeannie's condition worsened, and after six months she died. John could not have imagined a greater horror. He was paralyzed with grief. He would sit in the living room waiting to hear Jeannie's voice in the kitchen or expect to walk into the bedroom and see her standing in front of her closet trying to decide what to wear. The little details of her life were all around him, but she wasn't there. It seemed impossible, a horribly cruel joke.

The love of family and church got John through those days before the funeral and on that dark day of Jeannie's burial, but then everyone went back to their normal lives, and John was left to himself with two teenagers. The more John thought about how wonderful but short their life together had been, the more depressed and angry he got. "Why give me this beautiful thing and then take it way for no reason?" he thought. "Why toy with my happiness? What did I do to deserve this punishment?" "What in the world am I supposed to do now?" "What condition am I in to take care of my kids?" "Why do this to them?" He couldn't seem to turn off the questions, and each unanswered question just made him angrier. He couldn't stand going to church. He couldn't deal with all the questions and the well-meaning but stupid things people said. And he couldn't take singing songs filled with promises that he felt had been broken in his life.

Being alone made John angry. Being a single father made him angry. Seeing happy families together made him angry. Having to fumble through Jeannie's mail made him angry. His total lack of domestic skill made him angry. The people who said they'd be there for him but weren't made him angry. Lonely mornings and sleepless nights made him angry. His teenagers' constant needs and endless questions made him angry. Everywhere John looked, something seemed to stimulate his anger. And his anger wasn't just about people and stuff. John was angry at God. Sometimes he thought that God had done this to him for no reason. Other times he thought that maybe what he had believed was a lie; maybe there was no God, or if there was one, he was too distant, too uncaring, or too small to make a difference.

The truths that John had once rested in, he now hated. One night in a fit of angry despair, John grabbed the Bible by his bedside and with all his might hurled it against the wall. That Bible sat crumpled on the floor for weeks, a symbol of what was happening in John's heart. John isolated himself from his friends and gave up on most of his activities. He warmed prepared meals for his kids, but he ate alone and spent most of his evenings in his room watching TV.

It wasn't long before John's anger spilled over onto his children and his fellow workers. He blew up at home over inconsequential things, and at work he was earning a reputation for being disagreeable. Both his children and his coworkers avoided him as best they could but still endured the brunt of his anger. One evening John mollified his anger with a couple shots of whiskey, and it wasn't long before this became a pattern, and the pattern became an addiction. Most nights he went to sleep drunk and woke up hungover. His kids saw the empty bottles and the massive changes in their dad, but they were too afraid of him to say anything. They both were just marking time until they could get out of that mess and away from their dad.

The first DUI was a warning sign, but John paid little attention. However, his boss paid attention and told John he needed to get help. But the anger and the alcohol blinded John from seeing himself with accuracy. He told himself that what he really needed was to have the clock roll back three years and he'd be okay.

Finally, after losing his job and his children, John was forced to get counseling, and he made an appointment with me. It was then that the long process of change began to take place.

Freda had always been a bit of a loner. She never thought of herself as physically attractive, and she always felt more comfortable with books than with people. She thought she'd be single and fill her life with her career and church. Freda was an academic star, so she got a full scholarship to a great college and a full fellowship for graduate school. It seemed that she'd been right: her world was the laboratory, where she was a research star, and she found a family with her colleagues and the friends in her church small group. Freda was fulfilled in her work and had made peace with her singleness. Sometimes she'd feel lonely in the evenings, but Jack, her terrier, would jump up onto her lap, and the feelings would fade.

When Freda was promoted to a prestigious new research group, she thought the work and the people it involved would provide new companionship and deeper fulfillment, but she was in for a surprise. Freda would never forget the day she met Ezekiel. She and Zeke were given a project to manage, and they immediately hit it off. Their personalities were complementary, and their interests and training matched. Freda walked home from their first dinner together finding it hard to believe that she had met a man who not only liked her but understood her. Soon their relationship began to blossom, and before long they were talking seriously about their future. Freda had never been happier, and discussion of marriage became a regular occurrence when she spent time with Zeke.

Then the unthinkable happened. Ezekiel was informed he would be transferred to an overseas research group for no less than three years. It was devastating, but Freda told herself they could make it work. As the time for Zeke to leave drew close, Freda could tell he was struggling. Then the bomb dropped. In a tense, dramatic, and tearful conversation, Ezekiel told Freda he just couldn't do it. He couldn't manage a long-distance relationship for three years. He couldn't deal with the massive distraction it would be to the world that he loved. Zeke told her how much he cared for her and how sorry he was, but his decision was firm.

As Freda listened, she felt that she was going to pass out. It was like an unimaginably bad dream. The tears that streamed down her face as she was with Zeke became uncontrollable sobs by the time she got home. The next several days were a blur. Freda took long-overdue vacation days but had anything but a vacation. She felt toyed with and emotionally betrayed. She couldn't believe that Zeke could so easily walk away from her and the love she thought they had. She began to be afraid of the anger and encroaching depression that had taken control of her heart. She was aware of the bitterness that haunted her when she thought of how easily Ezekiel had told her he was done. Freda knew she was in a very bad place. She knew that she couldn't live this way. So she decided to run. She wasn't going to run away from her life and make a horrible moment even worse. In her suffering, she wasn't going to let herself run deeper into anger and despair. And she wasn't going to allow her heart to run wherever it wanted to go.

Freda knew she had to run to God. She knew that she couldn't handle on her own what she was facing and feeling. She knew the lies were too prevalent and the temptations too seductive. She knew there were traps laid in her path every day, traps of doubt, fear, anger, and despair. But she also knew deep in her broken heart that she was not alone. So she decided that she would run to her Redeemer. She would run to the comforts of his presence, his power, his promises, and his grace. She remembered that God welcomes the heavy and brokenhearted to come to him.

So Freda dove into the Word of God like she had never before. She ran to her small group, told them her story, and confessed that she needed help. She met with her pastor for guidance and comfort. She turned on Christian music the minute she got up to fight the darkness of heart that greeted her each morning. She fought the impulse to run from God and his people. She determined that rather than accusing God, she would trust him. She consumed anything and everything that would point her to the blessing of knowing God and being the object of his love and grace.

As she did all these things, she became more and more convinced that Zeke could take his *love* from her, but he could not take *life* from her. But something else began to happen: Freda was thinking about the people around her. She looked at people with new eyes and a different heart. She knew she wasn't the only person to face crushing disappointment. The more she looked and listened, the more she realized that she was not alone in her suffering, and the more she realized she was not alone, a desire to help grew in her heart. Freda wanted others to get the help she'd received and to experience the light of comfort that shined in the moments of her darkest despair. She had experienced God's comfort, and now Freda had become an instrument of that same comfort in the lives of others.

John and Freda, two people facing the unwanted, the un-planned, the unthinkable, but with very different experiences. For John, suffering was the context for the end of his street-level trust of God; and for Freda, suffering became the context for the deepening and maturing of her faith. So it is with suffering; it never leaves you the same. You run into the traps of temptation that greet every sufferer and are left with a cruel harvest in your heart and relationships, or you run toward the comforts of grace, which shine most brightly in the darkness of suffering, and reap a harvest of blessing. Yes, you may continue to suffer, or its effects may remain, but you now live with a changed heart, a sturdier faith, and a joy that suffering cannot take away.

Because there are traps of temptation that greet every sufferer, and comforts of grace available for everyone who groans in pain of loss, sickness, betrayal, and disappointment, and because the traps you fall into or the comforts you embrace will determine how you suffer, I want to invest the rest of this book examining both with you.

Suffering is dangerous because it exposes your heart to temp-tations as never before, but it is also a workroom for grace. This book is about how, in suffering, to identify and defend yourself against the dangers while you celebrate and seek the comforts of God's grace. May the result be more and more people whose suffering does not produce a lasting legacy of weakness and disil-lusionment but increased strength and greater joy.

Review and Reflect

1. Paul Tripp writes about suffering as spiritual warfare. How does this encourage you to persevere in your difficulties?

2. What are the implications of having a suffering Savior?

3. What is the "war beneath the battle" (p. 45)?

4. How is your view of God and his involvement in your suffering connected to your suffering experience?

5. Note how suffering can be a "workroom for grace" (p. 55).

Heart Reset

- Proverbs 4:23

- Mark 7:14–23

- Luke 6:43–45

4

The Fear Trap

I lay in my hospital bed not only shocked that I was there and facing what I was facing, but with a new hyperawareness of my body. Every little twinge of pain got my attention, anything out of the ordinary caused me concern, and everything the doctor examined or asked caused me to wonder why. My attention was captured by my physical state more than ever before. I couldn't help but wonder what would go wrong next. I became an expert in things that I had never thought about before. This new focus, this new awareness, wasn't a blessing; it was a burden. Suffering opens your eyes, focuses your mind, and produces awareness like you never had before.

After his heart attack, Brad seemed aware of every heartbeat and worried every time he felt a twinge of pain in his chest.

After her husband had confessed to being unfaithful, Sheila unpacked every word he said, examined him every time he left the house, and traced his steps whenever she could.

After Julie discovered drugs in her son's car, she became hyper-aware of his responses to her, the people he hung out with, and the places he went.

Sally had lost all she'd worked for. A victim of fraud, she now had her eyes open and found it very hard to trust anyone with her money.

After Jim's death, Linda couldn't stop thinking about all her loved ones. She called too often and asked too many questions. She just couldn't deal with the loss of another.

After being betrayed by his closest friend and colleague, Thompson watched others and listened intently. He told himself that it would never happen to him again.

After the accident that took his wife, Bill was afraid to marry again and was so hypervigilant on the road that driving became a major source of stress.

After losing his job, Frank became so focused on his failures and weaknesses that it seemed impossible to jump back into the job market.

Rather than joyful expectation, Mindy experienced her pregnancy with fear and dread. Her previous miscarriage had created a new awareness of the dangers of pregnancy and had robbed her of joy.

The death of his first church plant made Tom aware of things he had never been aware of before and wondering if a life of pastoral ministry was for him after all.

After being mugged, Sarah was so aware of everything and everyone around her in the city that she couldn't deal with the stress and moved to a distant suburb and a new job.

Sam wandered around his house, now more aware of Judy's absence than he had ever been of her presence. He was paralyzed, unable to move on.

Shuttled from foster home to foster home, Peter was all too aware that people often fail to do what they promise and do what they said they would never do. He watched every new family like a hawk and was unwilling to really open his heart.

Suffering of whatever kind, with whatever it may bring your way, creates a focused awareness that is part of the burden that every sufferer bears. It causes you to notice what once would not have gotten your attention and to carry concerns that you'd never carried before. This new awareness becomes fertile soil for a new set of fears that have the power to shape the way you interpret and live your life. Let me detail the awareness and fear struggle for you.

1. Your New Awareness Begins to Control Your Meditation

The level of wisdom of your interpretation of what is going on in your world and the sanity of your responses to it are shaped, controlled, and directed by the focus of your meditation. Since you and I never stop thinking, it's important to examine what is so powerful in our lives that it has the power to capture our thoughts over and over again. You know what it's like when something very bad or very good happens: our minds tend to return to it again and again in those moments when nothing else is commanding our attention. So our thoughts are always under the control of something.

Suffering tends to kidnap our thoughts and in so doing has a powerful effect on our emotions and responses. The dynamic is clear—the more you meditate on a problem, the bigger, scarier, and more unsolvable it appears. This is also why fighting for control of your meditation is so important in the life of every sufferer.

After waiting several decades for the promised son, the one on whom Abraham had invested all his hopes and on whom all the covenant promises rested, God asked the unthinkable. Had the long wait not been enough of a test? Was God really asking Abraham to sacrifice this long-promised son? (see Gen. 22:1–19; Heb. 11:17–20). Put yourself in Abraham's place. What would you have been thinking? What would you have felt? If all you focused on was the situation itself, it would seem like a cruel trick, and you would be filled with rage. And the more you tried to make sense of it, the more questions you would come up with.

But Abraham came into this moment having been fully persuaded of the goodness and faithfulness of God and God's willingness and ability to do whatever he had promised (see Rom. 4:18–21). He was able to calmly do the unthinkable, because for years his daily thoughts had been focused on the goodness, faithfulness, and power of his Lord. He wasn't paralyzed by the circumstances, confusing and distressing as they were, because he looked at those circumstances through the lens of the beautiful faithfulness and awesome power of God.

Contrast Abraham's response with the Israelite soldiers who for forty days huddled in their tents in fear of the Philistine warrior Goliath. Rather than reminding themselves that they were the children of the Lord Almighty, who had promised to defeat their enemies, and, in so doing, taking control of their meditation, they let themselves think about the impossibility of defeating such a warrior (see 1 Samuel 17). No wonder no one in the regular army volunteered to go into that valley and face Goliath. For those forty days the Israelite soldiers went undefeated by Goliath. Sadly, they were defeated by their own meditation.

The power of what you are suffering to control your meditation is a huge spiritual issue for every sufferer. What controls your meditation will control your thoughts about God, yourself, others, your situation, and even the nature of life itself. And as you meditate on what you are suffering, your joy wanes, your hope fades, and God seems increasingly distant. In the meantime, God hasn't changed, his truth is still true, and what you're facing hasn't grown bigger, but it all seems bigger, darker, and more impossible. Your suffering has replaced God and his truth as the lens through which you look at and understand life. You are not dealing just with what you are suffering but with the pain of how your meditation causes you to understand it, feel about it, and respond to it. When was the last time you prayed, "Let the words of my mouth and the meditation of my heart be acceptable in your sight, O LORD, my rock and my redeemer" (Ps. 19:14)? *What has control of your meditation today?*

2. Your Meditation Stimulates Fear

What you fear will be directly influenced by where you focus the thoughts of your heart. There is a direct connection between what you meditate on and what you fear. This is one of the reasons for the warning in Proverbs 4:23, "Keep your heart with all vigilance, for from it flow the springs of life." As with the other aspects of suffering already noted, the level of fear you experience when you are suffering is not just the result of the magnitude of the thing you are suffering, but, maybe even more significantly, the result of what has captured and focused the thoughts of your heart while you are living through it. The more you focus on the thing you're suffering, the bigger, more complicated, and more impossible it becomes. But something else even more significant and life-shaping is happening at the same time.

As your difficulty looms larger and larger, dominating the vision of the eyes of your heart and controlling the thoughts of your mind, your Lord seems to shrink in size and power. Few people suffer from the fact that their God is too large! Because your field of vision and the center of your thoughts are now dominated by your difficulty, God's awesome glory, the hugeness of his power, and the comfort of his presence don't. Fear then has room to settle in. Your suffering has already taught you that you're not in control, that you are fairly weak and definitely not independent. This means that in your heart of hearts, you know you can't handle your difficulty on your own. So it's spiritually devastating and emotionally paralyzing to fall into thinking that

God is small, distant, or lacking in the power that you know you desperately need. I've often heard sufferers describe how God has shrunk in their view, and I've thought, "If that's who I thought God was, I wouldn't trust him either." Because their formal theology hasn't changed, they are unaware of how much their functional view of God has, and because of this, they are chased and haunted by fear.

Because their meditation has robbed them of enjoying God's presence and glory, they are left weak, confused, and alone in their universe of difficulty. No wonder they are afraid! Remember, God will never ask you to deny reality, but if you allow your difficulty to control your meditation, you will end up hopeless and afraid. *What has your trouble done to your meditation?*

3. Fear Is Spiritual War

On this side of our final home, life is constant spiritual warfare. I am always a bit distressed when I hear someone talking of spiritual warfare as if it's the unusual, exotic, and weirdly dark fringe of the Christian life. The reality is that spiritual warfare is mundane, normal Christianity because our hearts are always a battleground between fear and faith, between doubt and hope, and between what is true and what is false.

So how do we become controlled by fear and how do we defend ourselves against it? If your meditation has begun to make you believe that God is small, distant, uncaring, or lacking in power, then you're left in the universe all by yourself. And if you're being victimized by cancer, racism, adultery, financial loss, death of a loved one, betrayal, etc., you know that you've no power to defeat it. No wonder you're assaulted by fear, if you've somehow come to believe that it's you against the world.

I've listened again and again to people of faith tell their stories as if God didn't exist. As I listened for even the slightest recognition of God's presence, promises, or power, I would think to myself, "No wonder this person is in such a panic." Problems have loomed so large that they've blinded them from the One who is their only hope.

It's important to remember that we were never created for independence. Even before the entrance of sin into the world and all the suffering it brought with it, Adam and Eve were designed to be dependent on God. Successful independent living is a delusion. If I think it's all on my shoulders, and I know that what I'm facing is beyond my wisdom and ability, I will be afraid. This is why the warning of Psalm 37:8 is so helpful: "Fret not yourself; it tends only to evil." Or, in my own words, "Stop allowing your heart to be controlled by fear because fear only leads to evil." The decisions we make out of fear tend to be the decisions we regret. You and I have to fight for the faith of our hearts. The next point will explain how to do that. *How many of your responses and decisions in suffering are made out of fear and no faith?*

4. Fear Is Forgetful

Perhaps there is no greater weakness in the heart and life of a sufferer than forgetfulness. Because suffering assaults your mind with so many new things to consider, to face, to decide, to wonder about, or to fear, it's so easy to lose sight of and to practically forget the things that have been your motivation, your comfort, your security, and your rock of hope. This is such a problem that the psalms, which portray for us the battle for a heart of faith in the midst of the trials of life, talk repeatedly about the need to remember. In fact, two psalms (118 and 136) are entirely dedicated to the importance of fighting forgetfulness. Hear the instructive words of Psalm 136, which I have copied for you below. If you're going to fight forgetfulness and the fear it produces, you're going to have to get into the habit of sitting down and recounting all the ways that God in love has guided you, provided for you, protected you, and met you with his grace and mercy. If you are going to fight forgetfulness, you're going to have to do this again and again. Doing so is not a denial of present difficulty; rather, it forces you to look at it through the lens of the presence, power, and love of your Savior. And you need to burn this refrain into your mind in those moments when aloneness, forgetfulness, and fear are about to set in: "Give thanks to the LORD, for he is good, / for his steadfast love endures forever" (Ps. 136:1). Stop now and read Psalm 136.

> Give thanks to the LORD, for he is good,
>> for his steadfast love endures forever.
> Give thanks to the God of gods,
>> for his steadfast love endures forever.
> Give thanks to the Lord of lords,
>> for his steadfast love endures forever;
> to him who alone does great wonders,
>> for his steadfast love endures forever;
> to him who by understanding made the heavens,
>> for his steadfast love endures forever;
> to him who spread out the earth above the waters,
>> for his steadfast love endures forever;
> to him who made the great lights,
>> for his steadfast love endures forever;
> the sun to rule over the day,
>> for his steadfast love endures forever;
> the moon and stars to rule over the night,
>> for his steadfast love endures forever;
> to him who struck down the firstborn of Egypt,
>> for his steadfast love endures forever;
> and brought Israel out from among them,
>> for his steadfast love endures forever;
> with a strong hand and an outstretched arm,
>> for his steadfast love endures forever;

to him who divided the Red Sea in two,
    for his steadfast love endures forever;
and made Israel pass through the midst of it,
    for his steadfast love endures forever;
but overthrew Pharaoh and his host in the Red Sea,
    for his steadfast love endures forever;
to him who led his people through the wilderness,
    for his steadfast love endures forever;
to him who struck down great kings,
    for his steadfast love endures forever;
and killed mighty kings,
    for his steadfast love endures forever;
Sihon, king of the Amorites,
    for his steadfast love endures forever;
and Og, king of Bashan,
    for his steadfast love endures forever;
and gave their land as a heritage,
    for his steadfast love endures forever;
a heritage to Israel his servant,
    for his steadfast love endures forever.
It is he who remembered us in our low estate,
    for his steadfast love endures forever;
and rescued us from our foes,
    for his steadfast love endures forever;
he who gives food to all flesh,
    for his steadfast love endures forever.
Give thanks to the God of heaven,
    for his steadfast love endures forever.

As you suffer, how well are you doing in your fight with forgetfulness?

5. Fear Becomes Your New Lens and Guide

I had never struggled with fear. Sure, there were moments of worry, but I never considered myself to be motivated by fear—until, that is, I faced life-altering physical suffering. Now, I have to say that there are legitimate reasons for fear. If as a parent you hear your child falling down a huge set of steps, the quick response of your thoughts and actions are all ignited by fear. In that situation, fear of injury propels you to provide rescue and care. But here is the issue: fear can be an appropriate response to the dangers of life in a fallen world, but we must not let it rule our hearts. Fear is a good thing in the face of danger, but it makes a cruel god.

No person on this side of eternity lives a fear-free life. No one always operates out of the rest and security of faith in God. Every one of us has moments in which we lose our mind and our way. So here is the thing that we all need to fight against: we must not allow fear to become the lens through which we view life and the guide for how we make decisions. I love the words of Jesus as he was facing the unthinkable: "Behold, the hour is coming, indeed it has come, when you will be scattered, each to his own home, and will leave me alone. Yet I am not alone, for the Father is with me" (John 16:32).

It is hard enough to be suffering but even harder to know that in your suffering, you are left to yourself to bear it alone. But Jesus did not give way to the fear of aloneness and did not let it be the lens through which he saw life. So he preached to himself the gospel of God's presence.

When fear rules your heart, you don't see or think about life accurately. You function with distorted vision that causes you to make wrong conclusions and bad decisions. And because fear distorts your vision, you trouble your own trouble. In counseling I have warned people over and over again that things were not as bad as they could be and that they could make them worse by responding to their trouble in the wrong way. So you have to fight to see life with the eyes of faith and not through the lens of fear. *Is there evidence in the way that you have responded to suffering that fear has become your lens and your guide?*

6. Fear Is Only Ever Defeated by Fear

The only truly practical and lasting solution to fear of situations, locations, or people is fear of God. Only fear of someone more powerful than what you are facing and the assurance that this One of scary power has chosen to unleash his power for your benefit has the power to give you courage in the face of something or someone more powerful than you. Fear of God, that thankful and reverential recognition of his glory, sovereignty, and power, is how rest and hope can be found in the face of what seems difficult and hopeless.

Proverbs 15:16 says it so well: "Better is a little with the fear of the LORD than great treasure and trouble with it." Fear of created things is a tempting trap to any sufferer, but trust in the Lord is a secure way to live. Fear of God does not remove suffering from your life but dramatically changes the way you suffer. When you fear God, the equation is not you compared to the size of your trial, but your God compared to it. God understands what we do not understand; he controls what we cannot control; he has power where we have no power; he gives what we could never earn; he is ever-present, ever-loving, and eternally gracious; and he pours all of what he is down on his children. It really is true that fear of God is the only solution to fear of anything else. *Where right now does fear of God need to overwhelm fear of anything else?*

7. Fear Is Temporary; God's Loving Care Is Eternal

Nothing that you and I face in this broken world is ultimate or eternal. It is important to recognize that what we fear will not last forever and that suffering, in the eternal scheme of things, will not last forever. God is eternal; his presence will be with his children forever; his grace is a gift that will never be used up or wear out; his power will never fade. In the final analysis your suffering will not determine your destiny; God alone does, and he is amazing in power and grace. *Where are you acting as if the thing you're suffering or are afraid of is ultimate and has more power to determine your fate than God does?*

Fear almost always accompanies suffering in some way, but it doesn't have to rule our hearts and decimate our hope, because, by grace, we are the sons and daughters of One who is greater than anything we could ever fear. He is in us and with us and for us and unleashes his glory for our good. God is the good news that every sufferer needs.

Review and Reflect

1. How do the biblical stories of Abraham in his faith and the Israelites in their fear of Goliath speak to you in your suffering?

2. Note what is controlling your meditation.

3. Slowly read Psalm 136 and, as Paul Tripp writes, "recount all the ways that God in love has guided you, provided for you, protected you, and met you with his grace and mercy" (p. 63).

4. What is your response to Paul Tripp's statement about Psalm 37:8, that fear leads to evil?

5. Paul Tripp states that fear in life can only be conquered by the fear of God. What does this look like for you?

Heart Reset

- 1 Samuel 17:1–58

- Proverbs 15:16

- John 16:32

5

The Envy Trap

Cat had been her most long-term and very best friend ever. They had known each other since grade school. They had participated in all the same high school activities. They had enrolled in the same college, declared the same major, and were roommates for three of their four years. They had found jobs in the same city and rented a place together, but in a moment on a horrible night, it all changed. Jude was on her way home from an office party when she was hit head-on by a drunk and unlicensed driver. She was in critical care for three weeks, then in a rehab facility for six months, and finally spent months as an outpatient learning how to live as a paraplegic, manage her wheelchair, and make the necessary arrangements for returning to work.

Cat was very gracious, loving, and supportive throughout the entire ordeal, practically living at the hospital during those first few weeks, but as Jude got better, it became clear that the place Jude had rented with Cat would no longer meet Jude's needs. Cat decided she didn't want to relocate with Jude because she was in a serious relationship, saw marriage on the horizon, and didn't want to move twice. It was a huge blow to Jude.

Those first few weeks in Jude's disability-appropriate loft were dark and lonely. She couldn't wrap her brain around what had happened to her life, she couldn't deal with the challenge of even the simplest of tasks, and she couldn't deal with the fact that it probably would never be different. Cat visited her often those first weeks, and those visits seemed like the only bright spot in Jude's life, but as Cat's relationship with George got more serious, the visits got more infrequent. At first Cat called if she hadn't visited, but the visits and the calls grew increasingly rare.

Jude felt incredibly alone, forsaken, and powerless. Meanwhile Cat's life became more and more fulfilling and exciting. George was a good man, and he loved Cat dearly. There was probably no harder day for Jude than the day of Cat's wedding. Locked in her wheelchair, she asked not to be a bridesmaid, and at the reception it killed her that she couldn't get out on the floor and dance. The night of Cat's wedding, Jude's discouragement morphed into something more dangerous—anger. It wasn't just the anger of discouragement and loneliness; it was the anger of envy. It had been nipping at her for weeks, and now it had her heart in its grasp. In the drama of her life-altering injuries, Jude made the huge spiritual mistake of looking horizontally instead of vertically.

Because Cat had been such a huge part of Jude's life, it didn't seem strange or dangerous to think about her all the time. But doing so was progressively destroying her hope and weakening her faith, and she didn't know it. There wasn't a day when Jude was free of thinking about Cat. She would be alone in her wheelchair in her kitchen and imagine that Cat was in her new house with her new husband enjoying breakfast. The more Jude compared her life to Cat's, the more she was eaten with envy. She envied Cat's marriage, her new house, her ongoing career, and, most of all, her ability to walk.

It wasn't long before the envy that had been reserved for Cat spilled over to everyone everywhere in her life. The more Jude looked around, the more she longed to be anybody but herself. The more she examined the life of others, the more she hated the wheelchair that she would never escape. She was angry that everyone around her seemed to have all the things she would never have. But it wasn't just generalized anger; Jude's anger had an object. In ways she didn't understand, Jude was deeply angry at God.

It's important to understand that envy never rests. Envy never lives in the heart as just envy. Envy quickly morphs into anger, the anger looks for an object, and finally envy shuts the heart off from trust in God. It wasn't long before Jude was no longer thinking about Cat; she was thinking about God. Why had God so richly blessed Cat while he had forgotten Jude? Why did he seem to hear the prayers of everyone but Jude? It made no sense that people who never paid God a bit of attention were blessed with better lives than she, who had followed him sincerely. To Jude, God now seemed distant, uncaring, and partial. She felt she could trust him no more.

Jude is not the first person to struggle in this way. The temptation to assess your life by looking horizontally rather than vertically is graphically depicted in one powerfully diagnostic psalm, Psalm 73. This psalm is a treatise on the heart-debilitating dangers of envy. Take time now to read through it carefully.

Truly God is good to Israel,
    to those who are pure in heart.
But as for me, my feet had almost stumbled,
    my steps had nearly slipped.
For I was envious of the arrogant
    when I saw the prosperity of the wicked.
For they have no pangs until death;
    their bodies are fat and sleek.

They are not in trouble as others are;
    they are not stricken like the rest of mankind.
Therefore pride is their necklace;
    violence covers them as a garment.
Their eyes swell out through fatness;
    their hearts overflow with follies.
They scoff and speak with malice;
    loftily they threaten oppression.
They set their mouths against the heavens,
    and their tongue struts through the earth.
Therefore his people turn back to them,
    and find no fault in them.
And they say, "How can God know?
    Is there knowledge in the Most High?"
Behold, these are the wicked;
    always at ease, they increase in riches.
All in vain have I kept my heart clean
    and washed my hands in innocence.
For all the day long I have been stricken
    and rebuked every morning.
If I had said, "I will speak thus,"
    I would have betrayed the generation of your children.
But when I thought how to understand this,
    it seemed to me a wearisome task,
until I went into the sanctuary of God;
    then I discerned their end.
Truly you set them in slippery places;
    you make them fall to ruin.
How they are destroyed in a moment,
    swept away utterly by terrors!
Like a dream when one awakes,
        O Lord, when you rouse yourself, you despise them
            as phantoms.
When my soul was embittered,

when I was pricked in heart,
I was brutish and ignorant;
    I was like a beast toward you.
Nevertheless, I am continually with you;
    you hold my right hand.
You guide me with your counsel,
    and afterward you will receive me to glory.
Whom have I in heaven but you?
    And there is nothing on earth that I desire besides you.
My flesh and my heart may fail,
    but God is the strength of my heart and my portion
        forever.
For behold, those who are far from you shall perish;
    you put an end to everyone who is unfaithful to you.
But for me it is good to be near GOD;
    I have made the Lord God my refuge,
    that I may tell of all your works.

In your suffering, can you find yourself in this psalm? Is there evidence that you have fallen into envy's trap? Consider what this psalm, which gives warning to everyone who suffers, teaches us about envy.

1. Envy Is Natural

Since every human being is an interpreter, every day we all do situational, moral, spiritual, and personal calculus. We are constantly adding up the details and circumstances of our lives to see the sum total of our beliefs, decisions, and actions. We're all spiritual accountants calculating the return on our faith investments. We all long for our spiritual investments and personal decisions to be worth something. Here are the big questions we all tend to ask: "What have I gotten in return for my heart commitments and life decisions? Has it all been worth it?"

Because these questions are in all of our hearts and minds, it's natural to look around at how others have done, but this is where we get into trouble. We'll never know the worth of our faith commitments and life decisions by comparing our lives to the lives of others. When we do this, we don't end up assured that we've made the right commitments and decisions; we invariably end up wishing for the life of those other people. We fall into thinking that the trials of others are easier and that the blessings of others are greater. So the natural response of those mistaken conclusions is to want what they have and what seems to have evaded our grasp. And wanting the life of someone else is never good for your heart and doesn't motivate you to continue to seek and do what's right.

2. Envy Makes You Question Your Allegiance to God

Thousands of disgruntled believers with envious hearts have spoken some rendition of the words of Asaph, the author of Psalm 73:

> All in vain have I kept my heart clean
>   and washed my hands in innocence. (v. 13)

It's so easy in the pain, travail, and exhaustion of suffering to throw up your hands and say, "I've obeyed for this? I've been a committed follower of God, and this is what I get?" There are moments in suffering when we're tempted to think that it's all been one big moral rip-off. We look around and it seems that the good guys are being hammered and the bad guys are being blessed. It seems that justice and morality have been turned upside down.

The flaw in this thinking is that it looks at faith and obedience as payments. It's as if we buy blessing by doing the right thing and avoid hardship by refusing to do the wrong thing. Our blessings are never payment for the good we've done, and our trials are never punishment for the wrongs we've done. This cause-and-effect equation is always bad spiritual math. We've all had blessing heaped upon us that we could never earn, and the hardships that God's children endure are the result of his love, because they are being used as instruments of his rescuing and transforming grace. Every good father does hard things with his children, not because he hates them but because he loves them and gives them what they need, which is not always the comfortable thing they want.

3. Envy Is a Wearisome Burden to Carry

Asaph says that his horizontal evaluation-envy syndrome was a "wearisome task," and it always is. It's adding pain to pain to allow yourself to fall into thinking that not only have you been chosen to endure hard things, but you're enduring those hard things because you've been wronged, that is, because someone else is enjoying the blessings that you deserve. It's impossible to think this even for a moment and not be angry. It's impossible to carry this anger for a while and not be spiritually depressed. Not only has your physical, relational, and situational world come crashing down, but you feel that you can no longer reach out for the thing you once thought offered you hope and rescue. Suffering becomes all the more burdensome when it becomes an indication that you've been wrong. Envy has never lightened the load of any sufferer.

4. Envy Ignores the Impermanence of the Comforts of the Present

Again, the words of Asaph are so helpful here: "Like a dream when one awakes . . ." (v. 20). That dream that seemed so powerfully real is gone the moment you open your eyes in the morning. The comforts and sorrows, the times of ease and the times of travail, and the easy roads and the paths of trouble are all fleeting.

What is will not last forever. What seems inescapable will not hold you forever. What seems to last forever will someday end. Envy paints the comforts of others as if they will be enjoyed forever. Envy forgets that all the things you envy are temporary.

Forgetting this is so dangerous because it distorts your value system. Forgetting the temporary nature of present physical comforts allows you to value them as much as or even more than the eternal blessings that are yours as a child of God, even when you are suffering. Envy tempts you to crave what is temporary while you devalue what is eternal. This never leads you anywhere good.

5. Envy Embitters Your Heart

Envy preaches a false gospel of favoritism and injustice, and because it does, it never comforts your heart. People who've been captured by envy seldom have peace, seldom have hope, and seldom find rest in God's care. The real burdens of suffering are made significantly more difficult when you carry them in a heart spiritually weakened by bitterness. Asaph confessed that he was bitter. His travail was not just the result of the hardships he faced but also of the bitterness of heart that made them all the more difficult to bear.

Bitterness is the long-term resentment that captures your heart when you think you've been treated unkindly or unfairly. The words of Job are a helpful definition of what bitterness is and what bitterness does:

> I loathe my life;
>   I will give free utterance to my complaint;
> I will speak in the bitterness of my soul. (Job 10:1)

First, bitterness turns suffering into a personal worldview. So Job isn't saying just that he found his suffering to be very hard; he's saying something much more foundational. He's looking around and saying, "I hate everything about my life." Bitterness now colors the way he looks at everything.

Bitterness so obstructs your view of blessing that you can't see it anymore. Bitterness in your heart is like being in the darkness of your basement on a day when the sun is shining and saying, "I hate the fact that I live in a world of darkness." You don't actually live in a dark world; rather, the structure around you and above you is obstructing your view of the sun. When envy becomes the soil in which bitterness grows, your suffering will become a lens through which you look at everything.

But Job says something else here that should get our attention: "I will give free utterance to my complaint." Bitterness not only shapes your personal worldview; it soon becomes an attitude of your heart. You no longer carry an attitude of hope, joy, or expectancy into the situations, locations, and relationships in your life, but an attitude of complaint. Bitter people don't have much joy. They expect and look for the worst and often find it. Bitterness puts a dark cloud of negativity over your life, and because it does, it robs you of your hope, and because it robs you of your hope, it erodes your motivation to do the good and constructive things that every sufferer needs to do so as not to lose his way in the midst of his difficulty. And a person without hope is not about to greet painful things with the courage of faith.

6. Envy Underestimates the Goodness of God

I sat with Sally and William as they told their story. They had been through terrible difficulty. There were moments when their story brought me to tears as I thought about what it would be like to live in their circumstances. Not only had life been hard, but it had been hard for a very long time. And not only had it been hard for a very long time, but it seemed that there was no way out. They were both depressed, discouraged, hopeless, and quite cynical. They didn't mind telling me that they thought that there wasn't much I could do for them. William said, "We've gotten a lot of advice, but nothing really helps, and nothing has really changed."

But as I listened to them, I noticed something missing from the way they told their story. The longer they talked, the more evident became this missing piece. It was so glaring that at some point, what they didn't say became as important to me as what they did say. Sally and William were committed Christians. They were theologically knowledgeable and biblically aware. They hadn't turned from their faith or rejected God in any self-conscious way, but when they told their story with great detail, there was no God in the telling. Years of comparing their lives to the seemingly easy lives of the people around them had completely blinded them to the presence and goodness of God. But as I listened to their story, I saw the goodness of God all over the place. From that time on, I was convinced that my job as their helper was to be a "goodness-of-God tour guide." I would lead them back through their story, and as we walked through it, I would point out all the places where God's presence and goodness were evident.

What could be more important for a person who's enduring the unplanned, the unexpected, and the unwanted than to remember the beautiful reality of the constant presence and everflowing goodness of God? When you feel unprepared, alone, overburdened, and besieged, what but God is able to give you reason to hope again, to believe again, and to live again? When hope in yourself, others, and circumstances has failed you, you need a rock on which to stand and a hand of help for which to reach. There is no rock so firm as the rock Christ Jesus, and there is no hand so strong and caring as the hand of the Father. Blindness to God's presence and goodness and to the caress of his grace only makes the heavy burdens of suffering seem even more impossible to bear.

7. Envy Forgets Eternity

It's hard for us. Suffering is so real, so physical, so emotional, and so life-dominating that it's hard to think of anything but the present moment of pain. Pain in your body can be heart- and life-dominating. It greets you in the morning, it nags you throughout the day, and it pulls the last groan out of you before you fitfully sleep. You can't run from it, because you have no ability to escape your own body.

The death of a spouse or a close loved one can kidnap your mind and hold it hostage. Everywhere you look, you are greeted by painful reminders of the person who once was. Everywhere you go seems to be dotted with memories of times shared together. A piece of clothing, a favorite book, a tree he planted, the song she loved, that picture, the piece of jewelry, or that thing that you just can't let yourself get rid of grabs your attention and pulls the grief out of you once again.

The pain of divorce can imprison your heart. Every morning you awake in that same big bed only to be confronted with the devastating reality that you really are all alone. You constantly feel awkward around old friends because you were friends as couples, and you feel as if you no longer fit.

All this pain tempts you to spend too much of your emotional and spiritual time and energy wishing for what once was and craving what others have that you've lost. Your physical pain reminds you that the people around you don't seem to have any pain. The death of your spouse causes you to notice all the couples that are growing old together. The shock of divorce causes you to wonder why they're all still together while you're cursed with being alone.

You're not aware of it, but your envy of others and the pain it produces lock you into a view of life that has a disastrous past and a painful present but is functionally without a future. It feels as if what is will always be. It's as if life has winners and losers, and you're on the losing team, and there's nothing you can do about it. But here is what's vital to understand, to believe with all your heart, and to preach to yourself again and again: *what is will not always be.* The biblical story is not an endlessly repeating cycle; the biblical story has a perfect beginning, a dark and painful middle, and a glorious end. There is a bright light in that dark and a painful middle in the form of the only perfect man who ever lived. He came as the second Adam to succeed where the first Adam failed. He won an eternal victory on a criminal's cross for you. This tells you that you're on the winning team. His victory is your victory, and that victory guarantees that the pain that now seems inescapable, you will not have to live with forever.

Thousands of years into eternity, as you're living in a perfect world that has been made new in every way, you'll look back on what now seems unbearable and inescapable as a brief flash of difficulty. It's hard to grasp, but try; there will be a day when you will look back at this huge and horrible thing, and it will look to you like a little thing. As Paul writes in 2 Corinthians 4:16–17, "So we do not lose heart. Though our outer self is wasting away, our inner self is being renewed day by day. For this light momentary affliction is preparing for us an eternal weight of glory beyond all comparison."

You see, you and I only ever really understand the painful trials of this moment when we look at them through the lens of eternity. This is one reason that envy is so devastating, because to the degree that it locks you in the cycle of daily comparing your life to others, to that degree it robs you of the glorious, hope-giving comforts of eternity. Eternity tells you that you aren't cursed with less but guaranteed gloriously more than anything you look around and envy in this present world. No matter what the next day brings, your future is bright, because a victory has been won for you. You can't let patterns of envy rob you of the comforts of eternity.

8. Envy Never Tells the Truth

It is so tempting, when you are suffering, to look around and compare what you are enduring to what others seem to be enjoying. And as you do this, it's so easy to fall into wanting the life of someone else. But as you can see, envy never produces a good harvest. Envy adds layers of trouble to the trouble you're already facing. Envy robs you of hope and destroys your ability to trust. And worst of all, envy steals away the hope that is only ever found when you're convinced of the presence and goodness of God. (I'm going to write much more about this in the second half of this book.) Envy does all this because envy never tells you the truth. It distorts your view of your life, the life of others, and the character of God. Envy whispers dangerous and debilitating lies into your ears. Envy never takes your suffering hand and leads you to the light. Envy never causes your heart to sing. Envy never points you to places where you are being graced. Envy points out all the bad things and puts its hand over your eyes so that you can't see the good things. Envy is a punch in the stomach when you're already out of breath. It's bad news when you already feel that you can't bear anything more. Envy is the enemy of hope. Envy is a mortal danger to be avoided.

When you're tempted in your suffering to look around and calculate, you must determine to look up and celebrate. When all you feel like doing is complain, you must require yourself to find reasons to praise. When you feel abandoned and alone, you must preach to yourself the gospel of the boundless, eternal, and unshakable love of God. For a sufferer, a heart free of envy is a spiritual war, and we must all cry out to God for the willingness and strength to be good soldiers. The battle for an envy-free heart is big and dramatic for every sufferer, but the grace of God is infinitely bigger and more than up to the task.

Review and Reflect

1. How is envy connected to suffering?

2. Why does a horizontal focus result in envy?

3. Where in your life is there evidence that you have fallen into envy's trap?

4. Explain what Paul Tripp means when he writes: "Our blessings are never payment for the good we've done, and our trials are never punishment for the wrongs we've done" (pp. 76–77)?

5. Where in your life is there evidence that are you "theologically knowledgeable and biblically aware" (p. 80) but your heart isn't fully engaged?

Heart Reset

- Job 10:1

- Psalm 73:1–28

- 2 Corinthians 4:16–17

6

The Doubt Trap

He slumped in with head bowed down, shoulders bent, and a blank expression, offered no greeting, and crumbled onto my couch. He was the quintessential image of a completely beaten man. Everything about him projected defeat, and it was clear that talking to me was going to be tortuous for him. His appointment with me was the only reason he'd ventured out of his house that day, something he hadn't done for months, even though he was sure that this too would be a waste of time, like everything else in his life had proved to be. He was broken, and his world was broken, and he was sure that there was no way that it would all be put back together again.

He had once been a young man with a bright future. He was the valedictorian of his high school class. He then graduated with honors from a revered university and ran through his masters program with little difficulty. But five years into a career that he thought would rock him to the top of his firm and his field, he began to have troubling physical symptoms. Within a year his life had become a drama of unanswered physical questions coupled with a worsening cycle of fatigue. At first he just felt unusually tired, but before long, he felt that he was dragging an unwilling body from place to place. Morning after morning it was all he could do to get himself out of bed. Dressing was an exhausting routine, and more and more his work performance suffered.

He was embarrassed and ashamed because he just couldn't cope with life. He wanted to tell his friends, but because the doctors couldn't find a physical cause for his fatigue, he feared his friends would think he was just emotionally and psychologically losing it. He reasoned that on top of the discouragement of his overwhelming fatigue, the last thing he needed was his friends to think he was a nut. So he began making excuses for not participating in all the spiritual and relational activities they normally did together. At first they pursued him, making sure he was okay, but after a while, because he never said yes, they gave up and quit asking.

After an extended sick leave, he finally went to his boss and told him that he was unable any longer to do what he had been hired to do. His boss was very gracious and wanted to help in any way he could. Even so, the thought of continuing to deal with the daily shame of showing up to work and accomplishing next to nothing, of being in meetings but barely able to follow the discussion, and of the awkward conversations at lunch were overwhelming. He was convinced that the only way out was to quit, and that day he did, much to the dismay of his boss.

That left him with only one reason to leave his house—church. He had loved his church and his small group and his circle of close friends, but what was once a source of joy had become painful. He began arriving late for church so he could slide into one of the back rows without having to engage in conversation with anyone. He hated being asked how he was doing or what was happening at work. He would leave during the last song or the benediction and get to his car as fast as his weary body could take him. But this didn't last long either. He would sit in the service with such anxiety that he could hardly concentrate on the words of the songs or the content of the sermon. And when he was able to concentrate, what was being sung and said seemed to address a different world than the one he felt trapped in.

After dressing for church one Sunday morning, he sat down on his bed to put on his shoes but simply lay back down instead. Going to church only left him more ashamed and discouraged, which was the last thing he needed. So he didn't go that Sunday or any Sunday thereafter. He was left with not only overwhelming and debilitating fatigue but an empty life as well. He had no reason to get out of bed, and even if he had, no reason to shower and shave. The Internet became his chef and butler, and when his home became too dirty and cluttered to live in, he hired someone he found on the Internet to bring order to the chaos.

In his withdrawal, he was left with himself. It's the thing none of us can escape. He had no friends, no work, and no church to distract him from or interrupt his private conversation. In his withdrawal, he had no one to talk to but himself during his waking hours. And because of his despondency, he found it nearly impossible to say anything positive to himself. Every day he talked to himself out of the darkness he saw all around him. He hated the brief success of his past, his present condition made him angry, and he dreaded the future. But at the center of the endless negative conversation was something deep and profound that drove him deeper into the darkness.

In ways that he was unaware of, his private conversation had become progressively theological. More and more, he thought about God, and because of that, the meaning and purpose of his life. But rather than letting what the Bible says about God help him interpret the overwhelming circumstances he was facing, he let his circumstances redefine his view of God. How could a loving God let this happen to anyone? Where were all God's promises? Why didn't God answer his prayers? Why were other people being blessed while he got cursed? Why didn't God use his power to help him? Why was God punishing him? Why had God turned his back on him? Why didn't God do something to help him? Why?

The Bible didn't answer his questions because he no longer had faith in what it said, and he knew that his pastor and Christian friends would offer him the same tired platitudes that he had once repeated to others in need. His love for God began to morph into anger at God. Worship devolved into an angry demand for change. The faith that had shaped his life now seemed to be a grand trick played on weak people. In his endless and dark conversation with himself, he finally concluded that if there was a God, he was not good or worthy of his trust. And in that moment he was all alone in his overwhelming and increasingly debilitating circumstances.

It was a miracle that he made it to my office. He told me about one friend who wouldn't be shut out, who would not stay away. It was a hassle at first; he just wanted to be left alone. He even hid in his bedroom when the friend showed up unexpectedly, but his friend would not relent. Finally, in an attempt to get rid of his friend by proving to him that he was okay, he let him in. Shockingly, his friend told him he wouldn't leave until he agreed to get help. So to get his friend out of the house, he agreed to one appointment with me. He reasoned that one hour of torture was worth it if it meant that his friend would finally leave him alone. But that one hour of "torture" was what the God he had given up on used to begin a process that would change him and his world forever.

There is so much I could say about the months we spent together, but I want to focus on one central thing. In the middle of his despondency and withdrawal was one fatal conclusion: he had quit believing that God is good. There is no deeper, more fundamentally life-changing doubt. If your life has been based on the assumption that God is good, and that because he is, what he has said about himself, called you to, and promised to do for you is reliable, then this form of doubt really does change everything. Here is why. If you've come to the conclusion, as the result of assessing your circumstances, that God is not good, then you will quit listening to what he says and going to him for help. None of us would ever think of seeking out the help of someone we no longer trust. Doubt in the middle of suffering has the potential to radically change your life but not for the good.

Let's Talk about Doubt

Like fear, doubt is not in and of itself a bad thing. God has given us the ability to wonder and the desire to know and understand. He has wired into us the quest to have our questions answered and our confusion cleared up. He created in us an intolerance of irrationality and contradiction. Doubt can cause you to ask profoundly important questions. Doubt will make you think deeply about very important things. Doubt will allow you to expose and reject falsehood. Doubt can ignite a life that is reasoned, wise, and protective. Doubt can keep you from being all too naive or an easy target for deception. Because doubt drives us to know and understand, it has the power to lead you to the One who knows and understands everything. Your capacity to doubt can drive you to God, but not always. This is why we need to talk about doubt, because this God-given capacity, wrongly functioning, can be disastrous.

There are two kinds of doubt. First is the *doubt of wonderment*. God's ways can confuse you. His ways are not like our ways. His plans often don't mesh with the plans we have for ourselves. What God knows is good for us doesn't always look good to us. He takes us places we would never choose to go. There are times when the way in which he delivers what he's promised looks to us as if he's breaking his promise. He doesn't warn us ahead of time before he initiates change in our lives. He doesn't invite us into the counsel of his secret will. He will not submit his sovereignty to our sense of what is best. He will exercise his power to deliver not what we want but what he knows we need.

Because of this, at street level, the life of faith is always a struggle of trust. In this struggle of trust you will be left with questions about what God is doing. If the doubt of wonderment causes you to come to God with sincere questions, asking is an act of faith. You're not rebelling against him; you're not running from him. You're not demanding answers, but crying out of your confusion for the help that only he can give. The doubt of wonderment is a normal part of a healthy life of faith. God won't always make sense to you, and when he doesn't, bringing your doubts to him is good. You see this beautifully portrayed in such psalms as 4, 6, 7, 10, 13, 22, 42, 43, 44, 69, 73, 74, 77, 79, 80, 83, 85, 88, 90, 94, 102, and 115. In fact, the vast majority of psalms were written out of a real-life struggle of faith. The doubt of wonderment is a normal part of a life of faith, and it's spiritually healthy when it drives you to bring your confusion to the One who has no confusion.

But there's a second and not so healthy form of doubt. It is the *doubt of judgment*. This doubt is not the result of wondering what God is doing. This form of doubt is the result of concluding that, because of our circumstances, God is not good and therefore not worthy of our trust. It's to bring God into the court of our judgment and determine that he is unfaithful, unloving, or uncaring in some way. The minute your functional theology tells you that God is not good, it's very hard to hold on to the confessional theology that declares he is. Once this happens, you no longer actually believe what you once believed about God, and because you don't, as I said before, you will no longer run to him for help. You don't actually think that he's with you and loves you, so you quit doing the "faith in God" things that you once did. Your suffering has told you that God isn't good, so you quit following him and relying on him for help.

I'm persuaded that there are many more sufferers in this place than we tend to think. I am also convinced that many of them don't know that they've reached these conclusions. The reason so many sufferers aren't aware that they've given up on God is that the process of theological change hasn't been self-consciously philosophical; it's been much more of a traumatic emotional-situational process. The surprise of situational distress has produced deeply emotional questions that have led them to deeply theological conclusions, but it's been nothing like the sort of theological debate found in a classroom.

As I talked to my depressed and discouraged friend, he described a God I didn't know, a God who was vastly different in character, presence, and power from the God the Bible reveals. As I listened to him, I understood why he no longer entrusted himself to the Lord and why he felt so abandoned and alone. It hit me that if I thought God was who my friend thought he was, I wouldn't trust him either, and I would feel that I had been lied to. But it is important to observe that my friend was seemingly unaware and unafraid of the radical shift that suffering had initiated in his theology. And he was also unaware that this shift in his theology was a major component in the decimating of his hope. Perhaps you should ask yourself right now, "What has my suffering done to my theology? What has it done to the way I view God and his presence, his promises, and his power? Do I still believe that God is the definition of what is loving, good, wise, and true?"

Sowing seeds of this second kind of doubt in the hearts of sufferers is one of the Enemy's most powerful tools. You get a glimpse of this in a rather curious passage in 1 Peter 5:9: "Resist him, firm in your faith, knowing that the same kinds of suffering are being experienced by your brotherhood throughout the world." Peter's first letter is written to people who are suffering, and as his letter is drawing to a close, Peter pens those words. Why would Peter say, "Look around; you're not the only ones who are suffering"? Is he saying, "Stop whining as if you're the only ones who suffer in this broken world"? Does he know that misery tends to love company, so he's giving them some kind of backhanded comfort here? No, Peter is doing something deeply theological and insightful. Peter knows that when we suffer, we are susceptible to the lies that the Enemy whispers in our ears:

"Where is your God now?"

"Why have you been singled out?"

"Perhaps God does have favorites."

"Why isn't God listening to your prayers?"

"Why do others have it so much easier than you?"

"Maybe God doesn't love you after all."

The function of all these lies is to sow seeds of doubt in our hearts when we feel the weakest, the most afraid, and are reaching out for help. The Enemy is seeking to make us doubt the goodness, love, presence, and power of God. He knows that if we begin to question God's character and power, we will quit going to God and seeking his help. His lies are meant to damage and weaken our faith so that on the other side of our suffering (if there is another side) we will not love and serve him as we once did.

Peter understands that holding on to a childlike faith in God in the middle of the painful experiences of life in this terribly broken world is spiritual warfare, and his statement is meant to give his readers weapons for the battle. He is saying, "Look around. Your suffering has nothing to do with God singling you out, turning his back, ignoring your need, or forgetting your plight. Your brothers and sisters around the world all carry their own package of difficulty. It's impossible to live between the 'already' and the 'not yet' without suffering somehow, someway.

Your suffering is not a sign that you've been forsaken; rather, it's a sign that you live in a world that doesn't function the way God intended and is in need of complete renewal."

This curious little verse isn't so curious after all, because in it are the wise words of a loving pastor who knows what his people are facing. Peter knew that the core attack against us in our suffering is not the attack on our bodies, our relationships, our possessions, or our circumstances, but the attack on our hearts. You can live well with a damaged body, but spiritual damage to your heart has the power to cause you to live in a spiritually unhealthy way. Peter's statement is intended to protect his suffering readers from the spiritual damage to their hearts and lives that results from concluding that God is not good.

The doubt of wonderment will drive you to God with normal, situational questions of faith and, because it does, it will strengthen your rest and reliance on him. The doubt of judgment will progressively weaken your faith until, in practical terms, you don't trust God anymore, and either you will feel alone in your travail or you will look elsewhere for hope and strength. It's practically impossible to suffer without doubt, but it's critically important to assess what kind of doubt has taken residence in your heart.

Fighting the Debilitating Power of Doubt

1. Fight the Devil's Lies

I want to add some practical counsel to our discussion about lies that lead us to doubt. When you are suffering, you have to force yourself to pay attention to your private conversation, that is, the words you say to yourself that no one else hears. We are always talking to ourselves about ourselves, life, God, others, meaning and purpose, relationships, trouble, solutions, hope, the past, the future, etc. Because of this constant internal conversation, we influence ourselves more than anyone else does, because we hear what we have to say more than we hear anyone else. Here's the question that everyone suffering needs to ask: "Has my suffering caused me to begin to believe things that are not true and therefore say things that are not true to myself?" You need to question your own assumptions. You need to argue with your own heart. You need to confront evidences of unbelief in your private conversation. Fighting the Devil's lies means being aware of the talk of your own heart and defending your heart against any perspective that would call into question the wisdom, love, goodness, grace, and faithfulness of God. Pray that God would give you insight into your own heart and the strength to fight this spiritual battle even in moments when you feel profoundly weak. *Have you allowed the lies of the enemy, whispered to you in struggle, to sow seeds of doubt about God?*

2. Count Your Blessings

There is no more powerful tool against debilitating doubt than gratitude. It is exactly at the point when you are tempted to think that you're not blessed that counting your blessings is the most important. A thankful heart is the best defense against a doubting heart. Recounting evidences of God's presence, his grace, his faithfulness to his promises, his provision, and the reliability of what he's told you in his Word reminds you of God's goodness, and because it does, it protects you against the lies that tempt you to judge him as less than good.

No matter how difficult and long-term your suffering has been, there are blessings to be found. As a defense against doubt, it is really important to give yourself to quiet moments when you look at the trail behind you and what is now around you for evidences that God is good and worthy of your trust. In other words, do what the old hymn says:

Count your many blessings, name them one by one
And it will surprise you what the Lord has done.[1]

If you can't do this alone, ask someone who knows you and lives near you to help you. It is an important spiritual blessing for every sufferer. *Have you taken time today to recount the many, many blessings that are yours as God's child?*

3. Daily Confess Your Struggle to Believe

In your struggle with faith you don't have to give way to the fear of guilt or hide in the humiliation of shame, because Jesus carried your guilt and shame on the cross. God is not surprised by your struggle. He knows the condition of the world he's placed you in and how those conditions impact you. He's never surprised or disgusted by your weakness. Instead of criticizing you for being weak, he comes near and reminds you that his grace is up to the task and, in fact, does its best work in those moments when you feel most unable.

So as the battle of doubt and faith rages in your heart, you don't have to run from God; he graciously welcomes you to run to him. When you humbly confess your struggle to believe in the midst of your suffering, God welcomes you with arms of love and blesses you with his presence, power, and sustaining grace. Since Jesus took all your judgment, God doesn't respond to you with judgment but with the faithful, tender love of a father. He welcomes you to be honest, and he will always respond to your confession with mercy. *In your struggle of faith, do you run from the Lord or to him?*

4. Get Busy

I find the content of 1 Peter very interesting. Peter is writing to people who are suffering through very difficult things. You would

---

1. Johnson Oatman Jr., "Count Your Blessings," 1897.

expect this letter to be one of sympathy, comfort, and encouragement, and although these themes are in 1 Peter, they surely don't
dominate the content; what Peter gives to his struggling readers
is marching orders. This little letter, written to sufferers, is a call
to pursue everything God called them to and blessed them to
experience between their conversion and their homegoing.

Rather than speaking just to the feelings of his readers, Peter
addresses their identity as the children of God. He calls them to
base their actions, reactions, and responses not on what they are
suffering, but on who they are as the children of God in suffering.
This letter is a call to Godward, gospel business. It's a call to get
busy doing what God has called you to do and to celebrate who
you are as his children. Sympathy is an appropriate response to
suffering, but the danger there is that too much focus on suffering has the potential to magnify its impact on the way you think
about yourself, God, and your suffering. So it's wise and loving
to encourage sufferers not to let difficulty define them and the
way they live. Godward, gospel-centered busyness has the potential to remind you of who you are as a child of God, what your
potential is even when you are suffering, and the things that God
has called you to that are eternally bigger than you and what you
are facing. The temptation when you are suffering is to do just
the opposite, that is, to quit pursuing all the good things God
welcomes you to and calls you to do in his name.

Good biblical busyness is a powerful defense against debilitating doubt. The more you give yourself to the devotional, dis-
cipleship, and missional things God calls all his children to, the
more you will be reminded of the enormous blessing and eternal
importance of what it means to be a child of God and a part of
God's unstoppable mission of redemption. In your busyness you
will experience God's presence and power, and you will have
the joy of looking back at the good results of the work you
have done in God's name. And the experience of these things

will work to weaken doubt and strengthen faith. *Has suffering robbed you of your enthusiasm to do the good things God calls all his children to do?*

5. Encourage Other Doubters

One of the most powerful ways to be encouraged is to encourage others. Perhaps my own story would be helpful here. As I was suffering profound weakness after undergoing many surgeries, and as I lived with the burden of wondering what would happen next, I met individually with young pastors each week. My goal with each meeting was to encourage these pastors who were struggling with the hardship of being young in ministry and pastoring struggling churches. There were mornings when the last thing I wanted to do was have that meeting. There were moments when fatigue seemed to make the next meeting impossible. There were times I did cancel, but in the midst of my struggle, I was determined to be faithful.

What happened morning after morning in these meetings is that I left encouraged. As I recounted to these young pastors who God is, who they are as his children, the amazing wisdom of God's Word, and the wonderful work that God has called them to, not only would they remember, but I would remember too. I told my young friends again and again that while I was ministering to them, they were ministering to me. God, in his goodness, was using something I found difficult to encourage my heart. What was hard for me to do (encourage others) became the very thing that God used to encourage me.

Who near you needs encouragement? Who near you has lost their way? Who is about to forget their identity as children of God and quit doing things that are good for their heart and life? You are uniquely positioned to help because you have a personal experience of what they are going through. You can speak into their struggle with sympathy and authenticity. You know the temptations they are grappling with because you have grappled with them too. In your weakness, you have powerful things to offer others who are weak.

You can remind those near you that they are not alone and, as you do, remember that you are not alone either. You can remind those near you that their suffering doesn't define them and then rest in the fact that it doesn't define you either. Every good thing you say to another, God will use to encourage you. *Who near you needs the very encouragements that you daily need yourself?*

6. Let Doubt Drive You to Jesus

I have said this before but will reinforce it here: in your moments of doubt, don't run away from your Lord. Determine to run to him. Here is his welcome to you:

> Come to me, all who labor and are heavy laden, and I will give you rest. Take my yoke upon you, and learn from me, for I am gentle and lowly in heart, and you will find rest for your souls. For my yoke is easy, and my burden is light. (Matt. 11:28–30)

Your battle is not just the difficult thing you're facing but the impact of the difficulty on your heart. Suffering can leave you spiritually damaged. Suffering can decimate your faith and leave you with life-altering doubts about the goodness and power of God. So in your suffering, doubt is a battle worth fighting. Remember, you never fight this battle alone but with the strength that is yours because of the presence and power of the One who gave his life so that you would have everything you need even in the darkest of moments in this fallen world. Cry out to your Lord. He hears; he really does. Run to him; he cares and will not turn his back on you in your moment of need.

Review and Reflect

1. How does doubt reflect our theology? Describe good doubt and bad doubt.

2. Paul Tripp writes that a "life of faith is always a struggle of trust" (p. 92). Where is this struggle most present in your life?

3. The apostle Peter writes that suffering is primarily an attack on our hearts (1 Pet. 5:9). How have you seen this in your own suffering?

4. Paul Tripp asks, "Has my suffering caused me to begin to believe things that are not true and therefore say things that are not true to myself?" (p. 96). What lies are you believing and repeating to yourself?

5. There are multiple ways to fight bad doubt: speak truth to yourself, count your blessings, confess your sin, keep "biblically" busy, encourage others, and be honest with God about your doubts. To what bad doubt are you drawn? Pray for the Lord's conviction of where and how you need to fight bad doubt.

Heart Reset

- Psalm 90:1–17

- Matthew 11:28–30

- 1 Peter 5:9

7

The Denial Trap

I had never seen him do this before; in fact, I didn't even know that he owned an exercise bike. There he was, riding as hard as he could as he told me that he planned to ride every day. You would think I'd have been encouraged and encouraged him in return, but I wasn't encouraged and didn't say much to spur him on. Seeing him on the bike made me sad because I knew what was going on. The day before, he had gotten a cancer diagnosis, and riding that bike was his response to what he had been told. He wasn't riding because he had a newfound commitment to physical fitness; my dad was riding to prove to himself that he wasn't as sick as they made him out to be. Like so many of us, he dealt with the devastating blow of that scary diagnosis by denial. I didn't know what he was telling himself, but I knew what his commitment to riding that bike meant. He rode to ease his mind and, in easing his mind, to give some kind of peace to his suffering heart. I was sad for my dad because I knew hope for him would never be found in denying the truth.

She had done it day after day, week after weak, and month after month. Deep in her heart she knew something was dramatically wrong, yet she worked to convince herself that she was mistaken and that things would be all right. Jared had always been a bit of a homebody, but he wasn't one anymore. His rare late nights at work had become an all-too-regular occurrence. The weekends away, which he once seemed to hate, didn't seem to bother him anymore. Charges on the credit card piled up, and there were overly friendly emails from a female colleague at work.

At home Jared had grown more distant and withdrawn, and their times out together had become more and more infrequent. Susan knew that something was wrong, yet she didn't want to believe that it could be happening to her. She explained away the changes, telling herself that she was making a big deal out of nothing. She told herself that every marriage goes through cold stages. She told herself that Jared had always been a hard worker. It wasn't until enough evidence piled up to make Jared's unfaithfulness impossible to deny that Susan finally admitted the truth. Denial had let her suffering fester and Jared's sin against her deepen. Whatever temporary peace her denial achieved, it left her with a bitter harvest in the end. I remember her saying to me, "I let this happen to me because I was afraid to face the truth about Jared and our marriage."

Sam didn't have it in him to tell his family. He had walked in that day as an executive with a zooming career and walked out of his boss's office unemployed. He walked away with a solid severance, but a day would come when those checks would end. He couldn't believe it had happened to him. He had been a loyal and productive worker. Year after year had brought raises and promotions. The last promotion gave him a larger income than he'd ever thought he would have. It enabled Sarah and him to move into a larger house with a bigger mortgage and to buy two new cars. Life seemed good until some executive in the home office in another city decided to begin the process of closing down Sam's division.

As Sam drove home that evening, he decided that he just couldn't tell Sarah yet. He knew she would panic, and if she panicked, there would be no way to keep this disaster from his kids. Sam was shocked and angry. He felt ripped off and betrayed. He had given everything he had to this corporation, and in an instant they had abandoned him. It incensed him that he had cared so much about his work, but they had cared so little for him. But Sam wasn't just angry with his bosses; he was angry at God. He told himself that he had been one of the good guys, that he'd tried to do what is right, and that he had believed that God would care for him. Where was God now? Where were his promises? Where was his love for his family? Where?

That evening Sam didn't drive directly home; he did something he'd never done before. He stopped at a local pub and had a drink. He told himself that he needed to tamp down his anger and clear his head. After the second drink, he knew he had to get home, but there was no way that he could bring himself to tell Sarah. When he got home Sarah was in the kitchen doing the normal supper routine and asked him how his day was, as she always did. Sam lied and said, "Okay. You know, same old same old," and quickly went upstairs to change. He sat on the bed determined to put on a good front. That night, after watching too much TV, Sam crashed into bed next to Sarah, who had no idea of the trial her family now faced.

Sam couldn't sleep, because all he could think about was the pending foreclosure on their house and the possible repossession of their cars. He knew that there was no way they could continue to afford the kids' school tuition, and the big special vacation that they had planned for years would never happen. He lay awake imagining that the phone would begin ringing with threatening creditors on the other end. It was a nightmare, and Sam felt betrayed, trapped, and alone. He looked over at Sarah sleeping and felt he had failed her miserably. Why had he agreed to the new house and new cars? Why hadn't he been more careful?

When Sam got up the next morning, it immediately hit him that because he hadn't been honest with Sarah, he had to act as if he were going to work. He reasoned he would spend the day looking for a job, and he would hook a new job and then tell Sarah. That way he'd be able to assure her that everything was okay. So he got dressed, kissed Sarah goodbye, and went off to "work." That day he sat at Starbucks and made several calls to potential employers, but in the afternoon he numbed his broken and fearful heart with three or four drinks. This became Sam's pattern for the next few weeks, and the nearer he got to that fateful day when the severance checks would end, the more he drank. Sam's response of denial had sadly morphed into a lifestyle of deceit and addiction. Lie upon lie marked his relationship with Sarah, and the daily drinks had given way to a bottle of whiskey in his briefcase.

Denial hadn't solved any of Sam's problems and only brought more for him to deal with, and it had surely done nothing positive for his relationship with Sarah. Sam knew a day was coming when the truth would be known. In suffering the loss of his livelihood and his ability to provide for his family, he had chosen a path that had damaged him spiritually and would soon do damage to his family, and he didn't know how to get out of the mess he had made.

The response of those people to suffering argues the point once again that it really is true that we never suffer just what we're suffering, but we also suffer the way that we're suffering. One of the tempting traps to every sufferer is denial. It is very tempting to deal with the pain of the thing you are suffering by working to minimize its size, power, and potential effect on you and your loved ones. It is tempting to work to convince yourself that what is bad perhaps isn't so bad after all. It is tempting to try to cobble together temporary peace of heart by some way denying the reality of what you are facing. It is tempting to rise to the throne of God, to create a world of your own making over which you are sovereign and that will work in ways that your real world is not working. Patients regularly deny physical symptoms, married couples regularly deny the true state of their marriage, and people in debt are often all too skilled at denying the financial disaster to come.

This may sound harsh, but it is something we all need to face: when it comes to suffering, no one swindles us more than we swindle ourselves. It is so tempting to tell yourself subtle lies in order to give some peace to your heart. It is so tempting to work at thinking that things will be okay that won't be okay. It is tempting to work to convince ourselves that we can handle things that are bigger than we are and beyond our control. It is tempting to put on a happy face when we are not happy and to give platitudinous, faith-sounding answers to questions, when inside we're doubting God's presence and love. It is tempting to deal with the hard things before us by closing our eyes. In suffering, denial is more of a temptation than what many of us think, while it's a response that never goes anywhere good.

A Welcome to Face Reality

I think it is very important for every sufferer to reflect on how utterly, unashamedly, and boldly honest the Bible is. From

Genesis 3 on, the biblical writers don't present to us a sanitized version of life. The Bible presents a broken world populated by fallen people where nothing or no one functions in the way that God intended. The world that the Bible presents is a world you will recognize, because it's just like the world you live in with all of its dysfunctions, disappointments, painful trials, and universal suffering. If you're looking for escapist literature, the Bible is not your book. From the shocking sibling homicide of Genesis 4, to the adultery of David, to the unjust execution of Jesus, to the final defeat of the Enemy, the Bible is marked by stories of deceit, family betrayal, political corruption, disease, famine, rape, murder, and unspeakable spiritual darkness. I have said this many times and it's important to mention it here too: there are stories in Scripture so weird and dark that if they were in a paperback book at your local drugstore, you wouldn't pick it up.

Why is this important to recognize? It's important because the honesty of the Bible about the true conditions we all face and are required to deal with is a gracious welcome for us to be honest as well. Biblical faith never, ever requires you to deny harsh and dark realities. Biblical faith never asks you to minimize your suffering. Biblical faith never makes you put a happy smile on your face and act as if things are okay when they're not okay at all. Biblical faith never asks you to defend God's reputation by acting as though you're doing better in your suffering than you are actually doing. God's honesty about life in this broken world is a welcome to each of us to be just as honest.

In fact, an entire book of the Bible (Psalms) is a script of the honest cries of God's people—cries of confusion, doubt, and fear in the midst of the painful trials of life. God never reprimands us for being afraid. He never mocks us in our weakness. He never minimizes what we're going through. He never turns his back on us when we wonder what he's doing or why we're facing what we're facing. Not only can your Lord handle every bit of your honesty, but his Word is a welcome to be honest.

So denial is never a biblical response to suffering. If you have to deny your difficult realities to obtain some kind of temporary peace, you may enjoy temporary peace, but it's important to know that you are not exercising biblical faith. You see, the message of the Bible is that the arms of God's power, presence, and grace wrap around the deepest and darkest moments of human suffering. God wants you to know that it's impossible for you to go through anything outside his understanding and care. The message is that God's grace is not just about your past forgiveness and your future hope but also about everything you're facing right now. All today's sorrows, disappointments, weaknesses, unexpected dilemmas, and the suffering that results have been addressed by his grace.

Crying out to God in your moment of need is like talking to a dear friend whom you are comfortable talking to because you know that she knows exactly what you are going through. But there is more. God not only understands the broken space that is our current address; he inhabited that space in the person of his Son Jesus. This means that the One to whom you cry has firsthand knowledge of the things you're dealing with. It is frustrating to every sufferer to share their travail with people who don't have a clue and can't relate because they have no firsthand knowledge of what you're talking about. Jesus is not just a student of our suffering; he became a firsthand participant in it. This is the powerfully encouraging message of Hebrews 4:14–16. Read these words slowly and carefully, paying attention to their implications for you in your present suffering:

> Since then we have a great high priest who has passed through the heavens, Jesus, the Son of God, let us hold fast our confession. For we do not have a high priest who is unable to

sympathize with our weaknesses, but one who in every re-
spect has been tempted as we are, yet without sin. Let us
then with confidence draw near to the throne of grace, that
we may receive mercy and find grace to help in time of need.

It is almost impossible to capture the life-altering glory and practical helpfulness of this passage for every sufferer. But let me
do my best to detail the powerful, antidenial implications of its
wonderful string of encouragements.

1. *In Your Suffering, You Have an Advocate*

You never have to tell yourself or others that you'll load your
burdens on your shoulders and somehow, someway, push your
way through. You never have to feel or act as if you're alone in
your suffering, because the One who sits on the throne at the
right hand of the Father not only faced all the things that you
now face, but he also faced the myriad of temptations that you
and every other sufferer faces. In your weakness, worry, doubt,
and fear, he pleads to the Father in your defense. In those days
when your heart is more given to anger than worship, he is your
advocate. In those moments when you question God's goodness or want what God has given to someone else, he pleads
on your behalf.

You don't have to deny what you are going through and the
way it is affecting you, because your Savior went through it too,
and he makes gracious arguments on your behalf. It's silly to
deny what your Savior already knows to minimize the power
of what he also experienced. Cries for help and confessions of
struggle are where true peace and true comfort are to be found.
Why? Because the One to whom you cry and confess has been
where you are. Not only will he not turn his back on you when
your suffering becomes a struggle of faith; in tender love he'll

take your case to the Father. In light of the advocacy of the Savior, denial makes no sense at all.

2. Because of His Advocacy, You Have Reason to Stand Strong

I think these words are so helpful: "Let us hold fast our confession" (Heb. 4:14). It doesn't take long for suffering, trial, and difficulty to become a crisis of faith. There are moments in suffering when God doesn't make sense to us. There are times when it seems that his ears are deaf to our cries. There are situations in which it looks as if his promises have failed. There are circumstances that don't look at all like good gifts from his hands. These moments can easily morph into a crisis of personal faith.

These words, "Let us hold fast our confession," are so helpful because we'll never get our reason for continuing to believe and to put our lives in God's hands from our ability to figure out our circumstances. We'll never establish peace of heart by trying to understand things that God hasn't revealed to us. Our motivation to stand firm in faith, even when we are going through things that we don't understand, is found in one thing: God's declaration of his intention toward us. In a hundred ways in Scripture he declares that he is for us and not against us. In the Hebrews passage he tells us he is for us as our advocate. He carried every bit of our penalty on the cross so that in our darkest moments of struggle, in the middle of the toughest moments of trial, we would be met with mercy, not judgment. That is reason to continue to believe, even when we are assaulted by confusion and fear.

3. Your Advocate Is Able to Sympathize with Your Weaknesses

Suffering always exposes our weaknesses. Suffering confronts us with how little in life we actually control. It confronts us with the vulnerability of our physical body. It forces us to face how quickly precious relationships can dissolve. It requires us to admit the limits of our personal and financial resources. And it makes us deal with the fact that we have little ability to get ourselves out of what we never controlled in the first place.

One of the hardships of suffering is profound feelings of weakness and inability. Suffering powerfully exposes our humanness. It reminds us that we are weak, small, and lacking in power and how limited in resources we really are. Suffering doesn't make us weak; it simply exposes the weaknesses that have been there all along. It exposes the delusion of our sovereignty and independent capability. It's painful to be confronted with who we really are and how needy and dependent we are.

This is where the redemptive fact declared in Hebrews is so helpful and comforting. The fact is that as you are forced to admit your weakness, you can run to One who understands that weakness at every level. The original word used for weakness in the passage pertains to weakness of all kinds. Maybe the best translation is that Jesus, our High Priest, is able to understand our "humanness," or the "human condition." Your Savior doesn't look down condemningly at your weakness. He isn't disgusted with your limits. Rather, with the knowledge of firsthand experience, he greets you not with abstract compassion but with tender, understanding sympathy.

This passage is telling us that someone knows what we are going through. There is someone who gets the burden of being a frail human being, making our way in a world gone bad. In sympathy he welcomes us to know that he knows, to be comforted by his understanding, and to not let the shame of our weakness keep us from running to him for help. He shared our humanity, he gets what we are going through, and he carries our travail in his heart. His understanding frees us forever from having to deny our struggle or act as if we're doing better than we actually are.

Jesus was born into the toughest of conditions; he was misunderstood, mistreated, and rejected throughout his life. His closest friends forsook him when the going got tough. He was betrayed by those he should have been able to trust. He was regularly hungry and knew what it was like to be homeless. He felt the sting of the worst kind of injustice. He endured torturous physical suffering. From birth his life was never easy, and his death was marked by public shame. No one rose to his defense. He not only suffered; he suffered alone. Even his Father turned his back on him in his deepest moment of agony. He did not use his power to make his life easy or to escape injustice and torture. He came to earth knowing what he would face, and he faced it all for us.

Don't let the fact that Jesus went through all of this without sin negate for you the real agony of what he suffered. He felt the full force of the same kinds of travail that you and I now face. And he didn't just live through this hardship; he lived through all of it for you, so that in your travail you would have a place of comfort and refuge to run to when there seems to be no one or nowhere to run for help.

The One who took on weakness is *for* you in your weakness, and that is the best of news!

4. You Can Come to Him with Confidence

Perhaps everything in your world seems to be shaken because you can no longer depend on things that used to be dependable. Perhaps what once got you up in the morning, motivated you to press on in life, and gave your heart joy has evaporated before your eyes. Perhaps what once seemed solid and permanent has eroded like sod on a wet hill. In those dark moments there's one thing on which you can be eternally confident and on which you can build your motivation and hope. It is the understanding and sympathetic love of your sovereign Savior. He not only has the experience to understand you and sympathy to help, but he also has the power to make a difference.

5. There Is Mercy and Grace Form Fit for Your Moment of Need

Almost every sufferer at some point is greeted by well-meaning people who want to help but don't really understand what the sufferer needs. Maybe you've been given food in your moment of trial, and you're thankful, but money was the real need. Or maybe people have promised to pray for you, and that means a lot, but you really wish they'd just sit with you and break up your long, lonely hours. Or maybe you're tired of getting advice, and you long for someone to just walk through the hardship with you. People mean well, but often they don't really understand what you're going through, and because they don't, they aren't able to accurately target what you need.

Again, this is why the specific words of Hebrews 4:14–16 are so comforting and encouraging. Because Jesus does understand exactly what you are going through, since he went through it too, he knows just what you need. So he offers you not a general catalog of hit-or-miss provisions, but help form fit to you individually.

When you are exhausted, discouraged, overwhelmed, and barely holding on to hope, it's tempting to work yourself into thinking that things are not as bad as they seem or that you're better off than you actually are. But because denial doesn't deal with reality but avoids reality, it never goes anywhere good. It will never give you what you need or help you be what you need to be when the unthinkable enters your door. But because Jesus walked in your shoes and faced what you now face, you've been forever liberated from the trap of denial. You're free to be weak and to cry out in weakness and free from ever having to put on a spiritual act.

The opposite of denial is not honesty but confidence. Hebrews 4:14–16 is meant to fill you with redemptive confidence, because it is only that confidence that can give you the courage to be honest with God and others in your time of need.

Review and Reflect

1. When you consider that "God's honesty about life in this broken world is a welcome to each of us to be just as honest" (p. 108), how can you be more honest with God in your prayer life?

2. Paul Tripp points out that when we deny our difficulties in order to feel immediate peace, we "are not exercising biblical faith" (p. 109). What does biblical faith look like?

3. How is your biblical theology challenged or strengthened by knowing that "God's grace is not just about your past forgiveness and your future hope but also about everything you're facing right now" (p. 109)?

4. What does it mean that "the One who took on weakness is *for* you in your weakness" (p. 113)?

5. How does living out Hebrews 4:14, "Let us hold fast our confession," help in times of suffering?

Heart Reset

- Psalm 3:3

- Hebrews 4:14–16; 11:1

8

The Discouragement Trap

I couldn't keep myself out of the hospital, and I've discovered that it's very discouraging to face a new surgery before recovering from the one before. I've been discouraged to have no control over things going on inside my body. I've been discouraged that I am unable to do what I've been called and gifted to do and, in healthy circumstances, am excited to do. It is discouraging to get up in the morning already exhausted before I've done anything. It is discouraging to cancel ministry event after ministry event. It is discouraging to be confused about what God is doing and why he is doing it. It has all been very discouraging.

In one way or another, at one time or another, discouragement is the experience of every sufferer. It is one of the burdens added to the burden of what's already being suffered. Beneath the suffering of physical sickness, loss, betrayal, or whatever other dark thing has entered the door is something way more powerful and dangerous. It is the spiritual war that rages in the heart of every sufferer. This is what I have been describing for you in the last several chapters. This war is a battle for the control of your heart, and whatever functionally rules your heart will then shape the way you see life and your desires, and it will control your words and behavior.

Let me say it this way: it's natural in suffering to have moments of fear, but it's dangerous and damaging when fear rules your heart. It's quite normal to struggle with doubt when unexpected, unwanted, or difficult things enter your door, but it is very dangerous to let doubt of God begin to rule your heart and set the agenda for your life. When you're suffering, it's natural to look over the fence and wish that your life could be as easy as your neighbor's. It's altogether different to live with a heart that's eaten by envy. So it is with discouragement. Of course, suffering is discouraging, but in the midst of your discouragement, it's vital to understand that discouragement is a major aspect of the spiritual war that lives in the heart of every sufferer.

The question is not just whether you are discouraged; the question is what you are doing with your discouragement. The question is whether discouragement is progressively taking control of the way you see yourself, God, others, your present, your potential, your future, God's promises and provisions, etc.

Jolene dragged herself to my office. As I walked behind her, it hit me that she even walked like a completely defeated person. It looked like every step took effort, as if she was pulling herself down the hall. She fell into my couch, and it was not so much that she had bad posture but that she had no posture at all. It was as if there was this lump of humanity in the corner of the couch. Of course, her head was down, and I think her eyes were closed, although it was hard to see her eyes. She hadn't greeted me when I went to get her and bring her to my office, and she barely responded to my questions. She was as discouraged as I've ever seen a human being.

As Jolene sat there and quietly and haltingly answered my questions, she didn't cry. She was way beyond tears, too discouraged to even cry anymore. She had no hope that talking to me would do any good. She was only there to quiet the people who had harangued her into my office. She had no hope that getting out of bed and doing anything would change her life, so she'd quit getting out of bed. Coming to my office forced her to put on real clothes for the first time in a long time. She had lost a lot of weight because she ate only when her husband or a close friend coerced her. When Jolene looked at God, she saw nothing to put her hope in. She had long ago quit going to church, reading her Bible, attending her small group, or even whispering a prayer here and there. Discouragement had cause Jolene to totally retreat within herself, and I wondered if I could ever get her to come out again.

Now, you may be far from where Jolene was when I first met her, but her story is important. Jolene is a picture of the damage that happens when discouragement begins to rule your heart and shape the way you see everything in your life. Left unchecked, discouragement will become your eyes and ears, determining what you see and hear and how you see and hear it. Unchecked, it will become the master of your emotions and the ruler of your choices and actions. Unchecked, discouragement will rob you of your hope and motivation. It will steal your reason for doing good things. It will rob you of your ability to trust. It will make you closed, self-protective, and easily overwhelmed. Discouragement will sap you of your strength and courage. It will cause you to see negative where nothing is negative and miss the positive that is right in front of you. If given room, discouragement will tell you lies that have the power to destroy your life. Discouragement is natural for someone who is suffering, but it makes a very, very bad master.

I want to unpack the dangerous power of discouragement by taking you to a discouragement story in the Old Testament:

> Then we set out from Horeb and went through all that great and terrifying wilderness that you saw, on the way to the hill

country of the Amorites, as the LORD our God commanded us. And we came to Kadesh-barnea. And I said to you, "You have come to the hill country of the Amorites, which the LORD our God is giving us. See, the LORD your God has set the land before you. Go up, take possession, as the LORD, the God of your fathers, has told you. Do not fear or be dismayed." Then all of you came near me and said, "Let us send men before us, that they may explore the land for us and bring us word again of the way by which we must go up and the cities into which we shall come." The thing seemed good to me, and I took twelve men from you, one man from each tribe. And they turned and went up into the hill country, and came to the Valley of Eshcol and spied it out. And they took in their hands some of the fruit of the land and brought it down to us, and brought us word again and said, "It is a good land that the LORD our God is giving us."

Yet you would not go up, but rebelled against the command of the LORD your God. And you murmured in your tents and said, "Because the LORD hated us he has brought us out of the land of Egypt, to give us into the hand of the Amorites, to destroy us. Where are we going up? Our brothers have made our hearts melt, saying, 'The people are greater and taller than we. The cities are great and fortified up to heaven. And besides, we have seen the sons of the Anakim there.'" Then I said to you, "Do not be in dread or afraid of them. The LORD your God who goes before you will himself fight for you, just as he did for you in Egypt before your eyes, and in the wilderness, where you have seen how the LORD your God carried you, as a man carries his son, all the way that you went until you came to this place." Yet in spite of this word you did not believe the LORD your God, who went before you in the way to seek you out a place to pitch your tents, in fire by night and in the cloud by day, to show you by what way you should go. (Deut. 1:19–33)

This story is placed for us in the Bible as a caution and a warning. Remember, God caused these stories to be written and retained for our example and instruction because these were people just like you and me. So that you'll get the full import of this historical moment, it's important to know the background of this story. After arduous years of trekking through the wilderness, the people of Israel were camped across from the rich and fruitful land that God had promised would be their permanent home. The report came back that the land was a very good land, but it was dotted with fortified cities and populated by people who were "bigger and taller" than the Israelites. And even though Moses reminded them of how God had carried them, protected them, and provided for them in the wilderness, the people of Israel were completely discouraged.

Why had God led them this far only to lead them into the hands of these powerful people? Why wasn't the Promised Land empty and ready for their move in? Why hadn't they been warned before? What were they supposed to do now? All the alternatives seemed bad. They could push forward, fight, and be slaughtered or turn back toward the wilderness and wander some more. It was very discouraging. Now, note that it isn't sin to be discouraged. We will all be called to deal with difficult surprises because God's plans for us are often very different from the plans we have for ourselves. We will all face "enemies" that are bigger in size and ability than we are. We will all be tempted to wonder why a good God would bring things into our lives that don't seem good at all. But it's important to understand that although it isn't a sin to be discouraged, what you do with your discouragement is deeply spiritually important.

You cannot choose to ignore the call to fight discouragement. In moments of confusion and weakness, it's tempting to give way to discouragement. It's tempting to follow the trail of its thoughts and desires. It's tempting to let it become the lens through which you view life. But every sufferer needs to fight those temptations. Discouragement is natural, but you need to know it's not your friend and that it always makes a very bad master.

I want to draw your attention to two of the most damaging results of allowing discouragement to take root in your heart in the midst of suffering. I want to use these as a way of unpacking the trap of discouragement and the spiritual war that lives in the heart of every discouraged sufferer.

1. Discouragement: Vertical Complaint

Let me begin with the bottom line here: discouragement opens your heart to a lifestyle of complaint, and complaint opens your heart to accusations against God. I have already said this, but I want to frame this discussion with saying it again: discouragement, for all of us, will be a normal part of the ardors of life between our birth and our homegoing. There will be moments when life seems impossibly hard. There will be moments when God confuses you. There will be moments of profound personal mystery. You will be discouraged, but how you face and deal with your discouragement will shape how you live your life.

When discouragement sets in and becomes the lens through which you see life, when it forms your assumptions about your life, and when it begins to shape your functional theology, you tend to complain. Chronically discouraged people find more things wrong than right. They tend to see more darkness than light, more trouble than mercy, more injustice than justice, more hate than love, and more rejection than acceptance. Although you're convinced that you're seeing life accurately, discouragement has distorted your perspective, and your assumptions about life have caused you to see one thing more than the other.

It's like when you buy a new Volkswagen. Suddenly it seems that there are more VWs on the street than ever before. You say to your spouse, "Honey, when we bought this car, I had no idea how popular VWs were." In reality, there aren't more VWs on the road; it's just that your ownership of a VW has opened your eyes to other VWs on the road with you. So it is with discouragement; it quickly becomes a lens on life. It predisposes you to see more brokenness than blessing, and it gives you ample reason for complaint. It won't be long, if unchecked, that complaint will become your default language.

What's the danger of a lifestyle of complaint? If you believe that God is not only in control of the grand movements of human history, but also in control of the particular details of your life, and if you believe that what is out of your control is under his control, then it is important to understand that there's no such things as a purely horizontal complaint. If I am complaining about the insensitivity of my physician, the lack of attention I am getting from my pastor, and the fact that my friends lack sympathy and understanding, I'm not just complaining about those people but also about the God who ordained all of them to be in my life. And the more I am comfortable with complaint being the normal language of my life, the more likely that lifestyle of complaint will morph into direct accusation against God. In the story of Deuteronomy 1 it didn't take long for that to happen.

When it happens, we've gotten beyond simply saying that life stinks; complaint has carried us farther down the road, where we say, "My life stinks because God isn't good." The God Jolene talked about was not the God of the Bible, but some distant, unresponsive, and uncaring being. And as I listened to her making accusations against the character of God, I understood why she quit going to him for help. "Because the LORD hated us he has brought us out of the land of Egypt, to give us into the hand of the Amorites, to destroy us" (Deut. 1:27). What a critique of the character and purpose of God, but, also, what a completely distorted sense of reality!

If you are suffering, and suffering has left you discouraged and more given to complain than praise, it's very important that you don't assume the accuracy and logic of your perspectives on life. If complaint has the power to focus your vision, it can also twist and bend your perception of reality and the God who rules it. In this way, every sufferer needs to have their assumptions about life lovingly challenged, both by the clarifying truths of Scripture and the loving corrections of the body of Christ. Maybe you don't see things clearly, maybe your assumptions aren't accurate, and maybe God is not who you've come to think he is.

I know it's hard, because everything I am describing has been my struggle too, but you and I need to be open and approachable in the midst of our discouragement. We'll never get the help we need if we first demand that people sign on to our view of things before we are willing to open up to them and listen to what they have to say to us. The Israelites were wrong; discouragement had distorted their view, and it was about to control the way they would respond to their leaders and to God. When discouragement has morphed into a lifestyle of vertical complaint, your responses tend to add another layer of trouble to the trouble that suffering has already brought into your life.

I plead with you to let down your defenses and open your heart. Could it be that in the middle of your suffering, there are ways in which you no longer see life, others, or God as clearly as you think you do?

2. Discouragement: Moral Paralysis

There is another subtle but practically powerful result of discouragement. First, it's important that we humbly admit that it is easier to complain than to praise. It is easier to notice all the things that are wrong or missing in our life than to recognize and celebrate all the ways we have been and are being blessed. Part of why we do this is sin—as long as sin still lives in us, we will continue to struggle with selfishness. The selfishness and self-righteousness of sin tend to make us think we are entitled and deserving. This selfishness tends to make life all about us—our happiness, our comfort, and getting our own way. We tend to dislike obstacles or living without something we want. I know I tend to want my desires indulged and my plans followed. I don't like to be disagreed with or told no.

Because our complaints are rooted not just in horizontal dissatisfaction (with people and situations), but also in vertical disappointment (with God), discouragement has the potential to become spiritually debilitating. We don't sufficiently consider the effect that complaint has on us and the way we think about and respond to our relationship with God.

Our willingness to do the good things God has called us to do is not first based on the promises he has made to us or the rewards he has promised us. Every good and godly thing we do is based on one thing: our trust in God's existence and his character. We only ever keep God's commands and follow his wisdom because we believe that he's good. If you don't believe that God is holy, righteous, just, loving, and merciful, you won't trust his promises or believe that he will deliver his rewards. A life of courageous obedience, no matter what, is always rooted in a heart that trusts God.

Discouragement that has become a way of seeing and has produced a lifestyle of complaint has the power to weaken or even destroy your motivation for obeying God. It has the power to rob you of the one thing, trust, that will enable you to continue to do good and spiritually healthy things, even difficult things. Complaint, because it tends to question God's goodness, faithfulness, wisdom, and love, assaults your trust in him. This is exactly what happened in the hearts and lives of the Israelites. Because they no longer trusted God's goodness ("Because the LORD hated us . . ."), they saw no reason to entrust themselves to him or follow his commands. So they took their lives into their own hands and rebelled against the One who had lovingly redeemed them out of Egypt and protected and provided for them in the wilderness.

If discouragement becomes a lifestyle of complaint, it can throw us into a state of moral paralysis. When that happens, we are stuck not only with our suffering but also with finding little reason in the middle of it to do the good things that God calls all his children to do. God calls us to do certain things that keep us spiritually healthy, wise, and strong. Sadly, I have heard it again and again as I have sat with sufferers, and I have felt the temptation myself:

"What difference does it make if I _____?"

"What good will it do if I _____?"

"It's hard to read the Bible when in your heart you're not sure that God cares for you."

"It's hard to go to church and sing those hymns and songs when they seem so far from what I am dealing with in my life."

"I can't stand going to my small group and hearing how wonderful those people's lives are."

"I don't pray much anymore because it hasn't seemed to make a difference, and I'm not sure God is actually listening."

"I know I'm supposed to be thankful, but I just don't find much in my life to be thankful for."

"If I had what they had, I would find it easy to worship too."

"I'm tired of hearing how good God is when every day I'm dealing with stuff that no one would ever call good."

"If God really loved me, why would he ever _____?"

"Every day I get up and I think, 'Where are God's promises now?'"

None of these people woke up one day and decided to quit following God. None made the conscious decision to reject what the Bible says about who God is. None said one day out of the blue, "I am going to take my life out of God's hands and put it in my hands and only do what makes sense to me." Their defenses were worn down by the burden of suffering, discouragement began to grow, complaint increasingly replaced gratitude, and before long they were left with little reason to continue to follow God in daily acts of devotion and obedience. As a result, they suffered not just the original difficulty but also the damaging results of no longer doing the good things that God has called them to do because he loves them.

What about you? Has suffering led you to a place where your trust has weakened and your obedience has waned? Are there things you once did with joy and confidence that you no longer do? Are there things you once did that you no longer do precisely because you no longer trust the One who called you to do them? Have you quit being motivated by God's promises? Have you stopped being emboldened by his presence? Are you no longer encouraged by his grace? Do you find it difficult to read his Word and pray? Is there evidence that the discouragement of suffering has weakened your resolve to do what God says is good even in times of disappointment, pain, and confusion?

Before we leave this examination of the danger of discouragement and its potential to leave a dark legacy in our hearts and lives, I want to make two important observations. I pray that these will encourage and motivate you to continue even when life is very hard. First, God is not shocked or surprised that you are discouraged. He doesn't wring his hands, wondering what to do next. He knows every struggle of discouragement in your heart. He knows your cries before you cry. He knew that you and I would be weak; that's why he promised to be our strength. He has promised never to give up the battle for our hearts until that battle is finally won forever. This means he fights for us even when we have given up the fight. Our desire to follow him may weaken, but he will never give up or turn his back on us. He knows us because he made us, which is why he sent his Son to be for us what we could not be for ourselves and to do for us what we could not do on our own.

Rather than judging you in your struggle, Jesus bore all our judgment so that in these moments we would be greeted with understanding mercy and just the help we need. And don't forget that it's impossible for you to be alone in your discouragement. Your Lord isn't just near; he actually lives inside you, and not only is his heart tender toward you, but also he has the power to enable you to do things that you could never do without him.

But there's one more thing. It is important to remember that the way to defeat the dangerous potential of complaint is not by silence but by praise. The more you commit yourself to counting your blessings, the more you will have eyes to see specific blessings in your life. The more you require yourself to rehearse the many gifts God has given you in the past, the more you will have eyes to recognize his gifts in the present. Pray that God would give you eyes to see evidences of his presence, power, love, and provision in your life right here, right now. Take time to think through all the good things you have in the midst of hard things. Get a journal and every few days write down things for which you can be thankful, that you could never produce on your own. The more your heart is filled with gratitude, the less room there is for complaint. The more you are given to worshiping God, the less you'll be tempted to accuse him. I have learned that no matter how hard a day is, there are beautiful things in that day that I should be thankful for, and there are reasons to celebrate the love of the One who gives them to me.

As you face discouraging and disheartening circumstances, may God give you eyes to see his hand of goodness, and may seeing give you reason to trust him and to follow his loving call.

The Discouragement Trap 129

Review and Reflect

1. How does slowly progressing, unchecked discouragement take control in your life?

2. Discouragement leads directly to complaining and can become your default language. How does that appear in your life?

3. Where in your life is there evidence that the discouragement of suffering has weakened your resolve to do what God says is good?

4. Paul Tripp reminds us that "the way to defeat the dangerous potential of complaint is not by silence but by praise" (p. 128). What are ways you can focus on praising God instead of remaining silent?

5. Prayerfully consider how discouragement may be impacting you spiritually.

Heart Reset

- Deuteronomy 1:19–33; 7:7–8

- Joshua 1:9

9

The Comfort of God's Grace

The more I listened to her say the phrase, the more it became clear to me that she was doing more than describing her experience. She was telling me who she thought she was. Her depression was no longer just a powerfully difficult and debilitating human experience; over the weeks, months, and years of travail, it had become her identity. "I'm depressed" was no longer an explanation of what she was going through; it defined for her who she was.

Now, let me say that long-term depression is horrible to live through. It has a radical impact on your everyday functioning, your relationship with God, and your community with others. It is a huge heart-and-life struggle that shouldn't be minimized, but it is very important to say that it is not an identity. The loss of a loved one, debilitating physical illness, a crippling accident, the adulterous betrayal of a spouse, sudden financial loss, the disloyalty of a friend or loved one, or the rebellion of a child are all very difficult human experiences, but they do not define you, and they must not be taken on as your identity.

In the midst of all the trials, travail, and traps of suffering, it is very important that we remember who we are and what we have been given. If we don't fight to remember our true identity as the children of God, an identity that nothing or no one can steal from us, our suffering begins to define us. Here's what is important about the identity struggle that lives in the heart of every sufferer: the identity we assign to ourselves shapes and defines the way that we live our lives. If "I'm depressed" becomes your identity, then in your personal life and relationships you will live out what that identity means.

The identity you assign to yourself determines three things. First, it determines your *expectations*. You and I were hardwired for hope. Whether you are aware of it or not, it is hope that gets you up in the morning and causes you to once again do the things you do. You hope that if you do _____ that you will receive _____ as a result. The way God has designed us is that vertical hope (our hope in him) would fuel a horizontal life of expectant faith and courageous action. Because we know God is good, that he is faithful, and that he blesses us with his presence, promises, and grace, we have hope that what he tells us to do will produce a good return in our lives. A joyful, obedient life is not just the result of surrender to God; it is also the product of hope in him.

If tragedy robs you of your true identity and redefines who you are, then it also dents, damages, or destroys your hope. When travail becomes your identity, it robs you of the one thing that all human beings need to have, what they were designed to be, and to do what they were called to do: expectancy. Loss of hope renders you weak and timid, lacking in motivation and courage. It causes you to hide instead of move out. It causes you to give up quickly instead of press on. It causes you to fear rather than believe. It leaves you convinced that you can't do what, in fact, you have the power to do. It leaves you with little expectation that your life can ever be more than it now is. Some kind of personal spiritual paralysis always results when a difficult situation becomes your identity.

But there is a second thing, and I have already hinted at it, but it needs further discussion. The identity you assign to yourself also determines your *potential*. We all constantly measure the potential we have to deal with the things on our plate. God means for us to define our potential vertically, to understand that our potential is vastly greater than the size of our independent collection of personal resources, because we have been connected to him by grace. When you live in light of your true potential as a child of God, you live with hope and courage even when life is hard. But when tragedy defines your identity, you vastly underestimate your potential, convinced that you're unable to do what grace actually makes possible for you. My depressed friend not only had very small expectations for her life; she was also convinced that she had little potential as a woman, a wife, a mother, a neighbor, a friend, and a member of the body of Christ.

When you have small expectations and have assigned to yourself little potential, in many ways you just quit living. That's the third result of letting what you suffer become your identity—it determines your *actions*. Why does one person step forward and face the hard thing while the other runs away? The answer is clear: one has hope and the other doesn't. Why is one person active in the middle of difficulty while the other seems paralyzed by it? Well, one sees his potential even in the storm, and the other is convinced his potential is small. The identity you assign to yourself determines how you assess your expectations, how you measure your potential, and how you act, react, and respond to your everyday situations and relationships. This is why it is so important to fight the temptation to let what you suffer define who you are.

The rest of this book is dedicated to pointing you to the expectation and potential that come with being God's child. We will invest this chapter and the ones to follow in a consideration of the comforts he gives, which suffering cannot take away and that shine brightest when your days are darkest. As you are suffering, the way to avoid adding more trouble to your trouble is to run away from the temptations we have already considered and toward God's comforts. Every one of these comforts is not just your hope as God's child but part of the reality of what that identity as his child means for you as you go through difficult things. These comforts are a more accurate description of your true identity than your suffering will ever be.

The first of these comforts is the stunningly encouraging comfort of God's amazing grace. Here is how Paul explains that grace to those of us who are suffering:

> For I consider that the sufferings of this present time are not worth comparing with the glory that is to be revealed to us. For the creation waits with eager longing for the revealing of the sons of God. For the creation was subjected to futility, not willingly, but because of him who subjected it, in hope that the creation itself will be set free from its bondage to corruption and obtain the freedom of the glory of the children of God. For we know that the whole creation has been groaning together in the pains of childbirth until now. And not only the creation, but we ourselves, who have the firstfruits of the Spirit, groan inwardly as we wait eagerly for adoption as sons, the redemption of our bodies. For in this hope we were saved. Now hope that is seen is not hope. For who hopes for what he sees? But if we hope for what we do not see, we wait for it with patience.
>
> Likewise the Spirit helps us in our weakness. For we do not know what to pray for as we ought, but the Spirit himself intercedes for us with groanings too deep for words. And he who searches hearts knows what is the mind of the Spirit, because the Spirit intercedes for the saints according to the

will of God. And we know that for those who love God all things work together for good, for those who are called according to his purpose. For those whom he foreknew he also predestined to be conformed to the image of his Son, in order that he might be the firstborn among many brothers. And those whom he predestined he also called, and those whom he called he also justified, and those whom he justified he also glorified.

What then shall we say to these things? If God is for us, who can be against us? He who did not spare his own Son but gave him up for us all, how will he not also with him graciously give us all things? Who shall bring any charge against God's elect? It is God who justifies. Who is to condemn? Christ Jesus is the one who died—more than that, who was raised—who is at the right hand of God, who indeed is interceding for us. Who shall separate us from the love of Christ? Shall tribulation, or distress, or persecution, or famine, or nakedness, or danger, or sword? As it is written,

> "For your sake we are being killed all the day long;
> we are regarded as sheep to be slaughtered."

No, in all these things we are more than conquerors through him who loved us. For I am sure that neither death nor life, nor angels nor rulers, nor things present nor things to come, nor powers, nor height nor depth, nor anything else in all creation, will be able to separate us from the love of God in Christ Jesus our Lord. (Rom. 8:18–39)

What is the nature of the grace that is ours simply because we are children of God? Note how Paul talks about it.

1. Uncomfortable Grace

In verses 19–25 Paul points us to two things that should bring comfort when suffering enters the door. Notice that from his very first words Paul assumes that suffering is not an unusual, surprising experience; it's the experience of everyone who lives in this dramatically broken world. Your suffering indicates that you live in a broken world ("subjected to futility," in "bondage to corruption," "in the pains of childbirth").

This means that everyone living between the "already" of the fall of Adam and Eve and the "not yet" of Christ's return will suffer sometime, someway. We differ only in the time and nature of our suffering. So suffering is an indicator of where we live but not an indicator of the failed love of our Savior. You haven't been singled out, and God hasn't turned his back on you.

But there is a second thing. In the middle of his discussion of the scary dysfunction of our world, Paul uses the words *hope* and *redemption*. These words seem to be out of place in helping people recognize the inescapability of unexpected and painful things. But Paul wants us to know that in the middle of the travail we all face one way or another, God is up to something good.

I know it is hard for those of you suffering right now to hold onto this—it has been for me—but it is important to grasp. God's grace often does its best and brightest work when things are the darkest and most difficult. God is both willing and able to bring very good things out of very bad things. The cross of Jesus Christ is the ultimate argument for this. What could be worse than the unjust murder of the Messiah? What could be more wonderful than Jesus's death for our salvation?

This side of eternity, God's grace often comes to us in uncomfortable situations and forms. In moments when we are crying out for the grace of relief, God is doing good things in and through us, using the very things that we want relief from as his tool. You see, God is so committed to his work that he will allow nothing to interrupt that work or cause him to turn away. In fact, he will use what seems like an incredible interruption in our lives to deliver the good things he's promised. So we need to embrace and encourage one another with the theology of uncomfortable grace.

It is so great to know that although God's grace often greets us in uncomfortable moments and ways, none of the things we suffer has the power to stand in the way of the amazing grace he's promised us. What a comfort!

2. Intervening Grace

Pain is painful, and it is painful not only in a physical, relational, situational way but also spiritually and emotionally. There are times when we are so confused that we do not know what in the world we're supposed to pray for. There are times when we are so emotionally distraught that the words just won't come. In my suffering there were times of unbearable pain when all I could pray was, "Lord, help me! Lord, help me!"

In your pain, God doesn't require that you pray biblically literate, theologically rich prayers. He doesn't reject your prayers because you don't have the right words, spoken in the right way. In fact, when prayer is hard, he not only doesn't reject you; he offers you help. And the help he offers is not a lesson in how to pray when it's hard to pray. The help he gives is himself, in the person of the Holy Spirit. When you don't know what to cry, he carries your cries to the Father. The Spirit, who knows your heart and what you need, turns your groanings into words.

You see, in your most confused and emotional moments, you are far from alone because God blesses you with his intervening grace. Verses 26–27 tell you that at the very moment you're groaning, the Spirit is representing you and your needs to the Father. God knows what you are going through and is not unkind so as to reject messy, chaotic, emotional prayers offered in your moment of need. He carries them to the throne of God where they will be heard and answered. When no one hears and understands your cries, in those moments when it feels useless to cry,

God listens, hears, and answers. He always greets your groanings without judgment. You don't have to rehearse your prayers, you don't have to wait until you're more composed and able to think clearly, and you don't have to worry that you'll say the wrong thing. Your Lord listens with a tender and sympathetic heart, and he makes sense of groans that no one else could ever make sense of. He answers not because of what's in you but because of the grace that's in him.

3. Unstoppable Grace

Verses 28–30 burst with comfort, but I am afraid we often miss that comfort because we misunderstand the hope embedded in these verses. Maybe one of the most misunderstood verses in the Bible is Romans 8:28: "We know that for those who love God all things work together for good, for those who are called according to his purpose." The misunderstanding of this verse has resulted in unrealistic expectations for many and grief and doubt of heart when those expectations are dashed. It is vital to understand that the only way to interpret the promise of this passage is to place it in the context of what the surrounding verses tell us. When you are reaching out for the hope of the promises of God's Word, its important to remember that Scripture interprets Scripture.

God is not promising in Romans 8:28 that all suffering will have an end in this lifetime or that it will end with some good result. This is not an "I guarantee you that everything will turn out okay" promise. The reality is that the unfaithful husband may not come to his senses and become faithful to his vows. That person who was crippled in an accident may never walk again. I may never again have my kidney function.

Many people have been led to believe that this verse foretells a good ending, and they have earnestly looked for it, only to face the pain of its never coming. If you have misunderstood the verse in that way, then how could you not conclude that the Word of God is untrue and that God cannot be trusted? In such cases not only do you suffer whatever painful thing has come your way, but you also deal with the grief and anger of feeling betrayed by God. This is why it is so important to know exactly the grace promised us here.

Notice that in verses 28–30 Paul isn't talking about your physical body, your situation, or your relationships; he is talking about God's relationship to you and the good he is delivering to you. What is that good, you may ask? That good is your redemption, the final completion of everything God has promised to do in you and for you by his grace. Now, it is hard for us when we suffer to understand what I am about to write, but it is so helpful. In these verses God is promising that nothing will ever get in the way of the most important gift we could ever receive. Nothing can stop the most important work that is going on in our lives. No good physical, relational, or circumstantial situation in this present life can be compared with the eternal good that God is doing for us and in us by his rescuing, forgiving, transforming, and delivering grace.

Paul wants us to know in our suffering that the best of gifts, the gift of God's grace, is never risky, it's never at stake, and there is no risk in trusting it, because the grace we're receiving today is but a present expression of a plan that was settled before the world was created. God's work is not a nervous response to what is going on in your life in the hopes that he can make good on his promises; everything he does in you and for you is the result of a gracious plan that was put in place before the foundations of this world were put in place, and nothing can stop that plan.

4. Providing Grace

As I was suffering things I never thought I would have to face, and as I still live with the results, I have turned to Romans 8:31–32 again and again. I love the logic of these verses and the hope they give for anyone whose life has been touched, troubled, and maybe permanently altered by the brokenness of this world. Paul argues that if God would willingly give us his Son, if he would control human history so that at just the right time he would come to live, die, and rise on our behalf, then would it make any sense for him to abandon us now? Paul is saying that in your weakness and need, when you are facing things bigger than you, and when you're feeling more needy than ever before, the cross is your hope and guarantee.

The cross stands as a powerful monument for every sufferer that God will go to any length necessary to deliver to his children the things they need. I do love the exact words here: ". . . will he not also with him [Jesus Christ] graciously give us all things?" (v. 32). There is nothing you will ever need that your Savior is not able and willing to supply. The cross teaches us that he will provide. This is not a wish and a hope but a statement of fact. If you are God's child, he will provide everything you need. The promise is not that your Lord will deliver everything you think you need or that, in the middle of your travail, you come to want. The fact is that your Lord knows exactly what you need, and he will provide "all things." The cross teaches you that you can bank on God's willingness to provide for you. You may be weak, but your Savior is not. You may be poor, but your Savior is not. You may be confused about what you need most in your situation, but your Lord is not. You may feel that you're at the end of your rope, but your Savior remains strong and committed to your welfare, and every day he greets you with his providing grace.

5. Inseparable Grace

The passage ends with a glorious grace crescendo. You can hear the redemptive orchestra swell as the timpani drums roll and the cymbals crash—hope and comfort build. With powerful and beautiful words, Paul declares that nothing in us or anywhere around us can separate us from the grace of God's eternal, life-giving love. It is music that every sufferer needs to hear. In those moments when you feel so alone, when you think that no one understands and you are tempted to wonder if God loves you, Paul says, "Yes, yes he does, and nothing will ever change that. Nothing will ever make him turn his back on you. Nothing will hold him back. Nothing will cause him to change his heart."

I am persuaded that there is a reason Paul gave this ending to his discussion of the comforts of God's grace to his suffering children. Think about it for a moment. There is a cry deep in the heart of every human being. It is the cry to be loved. What do we all long for but to be loved, not just on our good days, not just when we are strong, not just when it is attractive to do so, and not just in those moments when we feel we deserve it. We all want to be loved when we're weak, broken, confused, unattractive, and unable to love fully in return. We all want someone who loves us to hold us tight and never let us go.

We want to be loved when we have nothing to give. We want to be loved when we're confused and angry. We want to be loved when our suffering has rendered us self-focused. We want love that is sturdy no matter what, the kind of love you could never be sufficiently strong or good enough to earn. We want love that means, no matter the hardships that come our way, we are never alone. We want love that stays with us even when we're unable to dress ourselves up and present ourselves as lovable. And we want to know that this love is forever.

Paul says something radically encouraging here: the kind of love our hearts long for is ours because of our identity as the children of grace. The Savior loves us, and he will love us, and nothing can stop him. Nothing we could ever suffer has the power to constrict, obstruct, or end God's love. No matter what you're dealing with, you can wake up in the morning and say, "I may be weak, needy, and confused, but there is one thing I am sure of—I am sure that today I am loved!"

You are not defined by your suffering. Yes, you must work so that your travail doesn't become your identity. The things you suffer are powerful, difficult, life-shaping experiences, but they do not define you. If you are God's child, you carry the full meaning of that identity with you no matter how hard life is and no matter how weak you feel. Your identity is not the result of your circumstances or your achievements; it's a gift of God's grace. You didn't earn it, and there's nothing you can do to lose it.

Embedded in your identity as a child of God are wonderful comforts, just the kind of comforts that every sufferer longs for. We have looked at the first of those comforts, the comfort of God's amazing, right-here, right-now grace. As we suffer our way through this groaning world, we will never stop needing his uncomfortable, intervening, unstoppable, providing, and inseparable grace. And the good news is that the supply of that grace will never, ever wear out.

Review and Reflect

1. The apostle Paul writes in Romans 8 about inevitable suffering but also about hope and redemption. Why do you think God does not remove all suffering?

2. Paul Tripp makes a bold statement: "God's grace often does its best and brightest work when things are the darkest and most difficult" (p. 136). Why is this encouraging? Where have you seen this happen in your life?

3. How are you encouraged by intervening grace? When have you experienced it?

4. How is Romans 8:28 often misunderstood? How has this chapter reshaped your view of this verse?

5. Paul Tripp writes that our identity determines our expectations, our potential, and our actions. Where do you tend to find your identity apart from God, and how is it impacting your suffering?

Heart Reset

- Romans 8:18–39

- Ephesians 2:8–9

- 2 Thessalonians 2:16–17

10

The Comfort of God's Presence

It was a beautiful, comforting picture of faithful love. I didn't ask her to do it; I didn't know she would offer to do it. It was much more of a wonderful portrait of her heart than it was of my need. She did it because of what was in her, not because of what she had gotten for me. In those first scary and torturous days in the hospital, Luella never left my side. It wasn't just that she was there during normal visiting hours to talk with doctors and to greet the visitors whom I was unable to greet. She slept next to me in an uncomfortable recliner every night. When the spasms returned, the pain intensified, or the nurse awakened me for medication, Luella was with me. In the morning when I awoke to face a day I really didn't want to face, Luella was right there with me. When tears came, she was there to comfort. When I got discouraged, she was quick to encourage.

I was comforted by more than words. I was comforted by her presence and what her presence said about her love for me. She had put her world on hold for my sake. I have thought many times since that Luella's faithful, attentive presence in the darkest of days and the weakest of moments is a beautiful picture of the faithful presence of another. God is the ultimate present one. He has invaded my life by his grace. He is with me, for me, and in me. The hope I have is more than a theological system or wisdom principles for everyday life. My hope rests on the willing, faithful, powerful, and loving presence of God with me. It is the ultimate gift of gifts to everyone who walks the harsh and bumpy road between birth and eternity. God has given us no sweeter, more beautiful gift than the gift of himself. He is the gift that changes everything. His presence is what every sufferer needs, whether they know it or not.

I love how David begins Psalm 27, a psalm that was written during dark days in his life. It is a psalm of trouble, but it doesn't begin with trouble; it begins with wonderful, mind-expanding, heart-engaging, life-changing theology. And there's a lesson in this. It is never more important than in times of suffering to hold onto and remember the theology of the Word of God. When you are suffering, it is vital that you preach regularly to yourself the truths that Scripture declares. It is vital that your thinking, feeling, interpreting, and craving heart is given the wisdom, guidance, and comfort that only the theology of the Word of God can give. Bad theology will complicate and worsen your suffering. Bad theology will crush your hope when it needs to be bolstered. Bad theology will weaken your faith when it needs to be strengthened. Bad theology will leave your heart wondering and wandering, when it needs to be rooted and at peace. I would ask you, when suffering enters your door, where does your heart run? What do you fill your mind with?

Let me look at the first verse of Psalm 27 with you:

The LORD is my light and my salvation;
    whom shall I fear?
The LORD is the stronghold of my life;
    of whom shall I be afraid?

Notice the theology presented in this verse. David's hope as he faces the unthinkable is not an abstract, distant, or impersonal set of ideas. The theology that he preaches to himself in this psalm rests its entire hope on the presence and grace of a person. To leave out the "my" and shorten his declaration to simply, "The LORD is light," would take away the personal power and majesty from the theological declaration. In fact, look anywhere in Scripture and you'll see that the theology of the Word of God is never presented in an academic, impersonal, abstract way. The epicenter of the Bible's theology is the story of God coming to dwell with his people and unleashing his glory for their good.

Here David celebrates the only place he can find hope—in the presence of the Lord. To be David's light, salvation, and stronghold, the Lord must be near. In the pain of unthinkable things David says, "God, it's your presence that lights my way, it's your presence that gives me hope that I will be delivered from evil, and it's your presence that provides refuge for me when it seems that there is nowhere to run." When we are facing hardship, it is vital that we preach to ourselves the theology of the presence of the Lord. That theology doesn't just define the nature of God's commitment to us; it also defines who we are as children of God. Psalm 27:1 defines David's identity more clearly and accurately than any circumstance or relationship ever could. We were wired to get our identity vertically, because the things we look to horizontally will never deliver to us the security of identity that we find in the presence and grace of God.

Our hope is not found in understanding why God allowed suffering into our lives. Our hope is not found in the belief that somehow we will tough our way through. Our hope is not found in doctors, lawyers, pastors, family, or friends. Our hope is not found in our resilience or ingenuity. Our hope is not found in ideas or things. Though we may look to all those for temporary help, ultimately our hope rests in the faithful and gracious presence of the Lord with us.

He is not weakened by what weakens us. He is not confused by what confuses us. He does not suffer from the mood swings that afflict us. He is not afraid like we are. He never makes a bad decision. He never finds himself out of control. He never wants to take back his words. He never regrets the way he's behaved. He never responds impulsively. His choices are never driven by anxiety. He never dreads the next day. He never wants to give up. He is never frustrated by an inability to make a difference. He is with us, but the reason this is so wonderfully comforting is that he is completely unlike us in every way. He is limitless in power, he has authority over everything, he is perfect in every way, he dwells with us, and he assures us that he's not leaving.

I want to direct your attention to two amazing promises about God's presence that provide true, lasting, and sturdy hope when things you have hoped in lie beaten, battered, and broken into pieces. When the confusion of the unexpected so controls your mind that you are barely able to think, these promises can give you clarity. When weakness seems to make everything in your life hard or nearly impossible, these promises can renew your strength. When the betrayal of a loved one or the uniqueness of your suffering makes you feel completely alienated and alone, these promises will remind you that there is someone who holds you close. When it seems as if you lack the resources you need to deal with what you are facing, these promises remind you that you have more, much more, potential than you would have on your own. When darkness has enveloped you, and you feel that you're stumbling around in the night, these promises have the power to illumine your way.

In a moment your life can change dramatically. In a moment the future that seemed so sure evaporates before your eyes. In a moment that loved one whom you thought would walk with you for the rest of your days walks away or is taken away, never to return again. In a single conversation you are told that sickness will rob you of your physical vitality. In a moment an injury changes your life forever. Yes, life changes in little ordinary moments or in dramatic big moments. You and I have no power to make our lives stay as they are. We have no power to welcome only the good things into our lives and ward off the bad things. We cannot assure ourselves that we will always be loved, protected, and healthy or will always have the resources we need. We cannot put security systems in our lives to protect us from fear and sorrow. When we're going through dark and tough things, we cannot guarantee ourselves that these will pass and that things will get better. We're all dealing with forces bigger and more powerful than we are. It only takes the wicked whip of a tornado or the fearsome power of a hurricane to remind us of how small we are, how fragile our lives are, and how little power we actually have.

I have had the privilege of listening to fellow sufferers as they describe their inability to control their circumstances. One dear lady described it this way: "Paul, I feel that I'm sliding down a long, long mud tube. I don't know where it's going or if it's ever going to end, but there are no handholds to grab that would keep me from sliding down even more." That's a powerful picture of a scary human experience. A man captured it this way for me: "It's like I've been locked in a very small box. There are no holes where I can look out. There is no way to get out, and I just sit in the box wondering if this is going to be it for me." Imagine getting up every day to the mud tube or the locked box, or maybe that is what you get up to.

I want, in these moments, to help you do more than find ways to escape or survive. I want to help you understand that these moments have the unique power to transform you. In fact, I argue that moments of suffering are always transformational in some way. No one ever comes out of the unexpected, the unwanted, the difficult, and the discouraging unchanged. What you suffer will change you. You will not rise out of tragedy the way you were before it overtook you.

You might come out of suffering angry, doubtful, self-protective, cynical, or bitter, or allow it to make you that way. You might feel forsaken and ripped off, and although you never talk about it, you take spiritual and emotional scars into every situation and relationship thereafter. You may not see it or be willing to admit it, but you've changed, and the results are tragic.

Alternatively, suffering can form in you new and beautiful things, things that grow only from the soil of difficulty. Suffering has the power not only to renew your hope but also to transform it. Suffering can give you a type of strength unrelated to your gifts, health, power, or position. Suffering has the power to help you see where you've been completely blind but didn't know it. Suffering can bless you with a joy that's independent of life being easy and people liking you. Suffering has the power to turn your timidity into courage and your doubt into surety. Hardship can turn envy into contentment and complaint into praise. It has the power to make you tender and approachable, to replace subtle rebellion with joyful surrender. Suffering has the power to form beautiful things in your heart that reform the way you live your life. It has incredible power to be a tool of transforming grace.

You may be thinking, "Paul, are you ever going to get to talking about these two amazing promises?" The reason I've taken time to introduce them is that acknowledging the inescapability of suffering's effects provides a reason for every sufferer to get excited about understanding the full meaning and import of the two promises of God's presence at the heart of the right-here, right-now hope of the gospel.

"I Am with You Always"

There could be no more stunning declaration packed with more practical hope than the words "I am with you always."

These words portray a reality so glorious that it is impossible to overstate its magnitude. It is the ultimate game changer. It is the best of all good news. These words carry with them help and comfort that can be found nowhere else. And important here is that these words express more than a promise; they capture a state of being for every believer living through the harsh things.

"And behold, I am with you always" (Matt. 28:20). It is important to note that Jesus spoke these words to his disciples while they were being commissioned to give their lives as agents of his great redemptive mission. Jesus ended his commission with these words because he knew the world he was sending his disciples into, and he knew what they would face. He knew that their way would be difficult and their job uncomfortable. He knew that they would face constant opposition, misunderstanding, accusation, and rejection. He knew that they would be chased and imprisoned, persecuted and beaten, and that many of them would give their lives for his cause.

What's important to understand, for our purposes, about the context of these beautiful words is that they were spoken to give comfort to sufferers. Jesus was commissioning his own to suffer for his sake. But he would not let them suffer alone. He would not let them suffer in their own strength. He would not leave them to their own political standing. He would not let them rely on their own wisdom. He would give these loyal suffering ones the best assurance ever—that he would always be with them. He would not think of sending them into the cruelty of this fallen world without going with them. He knew what they were facing, and he would give them what they needed, and, more than anything else, what they needed was him.

There are times when we try to comfort or assure a sufferer with words. We try to say just the right thing:

"I really do care for you."

"I'm so sorry you have to deal with this."

"I am there for you."

"You're surrounded by people who love you."

"There'll be a light at the end of this tunnel."

"This too will pass."

When we say these things, we are sincere and well intentioned, but the words tend to ring empty. The reason is that they are spoken by frail human beings who have little ability to alter the circumstances that are causing the suffering. We can be sympathetic, we can help in certain ways, but our potential to make a significant difference is very limited. We look for things to say because we don't know what else to do.

But it is not so with God. His words are never empty but carry a level of power and authority that's hard for us to grasp. When, in your suffering, you reflect on the words, "I am with you always," remember that these words are spoken by the God of Isaiah 40. Take time now to read it.

In Isaiah 40 the prophet stretches human language as far as he can to somehow, someway help us get just a little picture of the magnitude of God's grandeur and love. God is not like us. He is the definition of wisdom, faithfulness, power, and love. There is nothing or no one not under his rule. And he exercises his power so that we will never, ever be left alone. As we noted earlier, you can be stripped of everything in life on which you've depended and not have lost everything, because it is impossible for any of God's children, no matter what is going on, to lose him.

Now, a little bit of biblical history would be helpful here. In the Old Testament God promised to be with his children, but that promise meant something different then than it does today. When the tabernacle was built, the shekinah glory of God filled the Most Holy Place. God, in a cloud of glory, made his physical presence visible. In a real way, the tabernacle was his residence among his people. This meant that he was present with his people, but to experience his presence, they had to go to where he was. But in the New Testament when Jesus speaks to his disciples of his presence, he is alerting them to what would happen as the result of his life, death, and resurrection. No longer would his children need to go to the temple to experience his presence; instead, his people would become the place where he lives.

Yes, it is true—if you are God's child, he has unbuttoned you and gotten inside of you. We don't have to go where God is, because we are where he is. Whether you sense it or not, he lives in you. Whether or not you have sought his help on a particular day, he lives inside you. Whether, in your suffering, you have forgotten, ignored, or gotten mad at him, he lives inside you. Whether in your travail you have run to him or attempted to run from him, he lives inside you. There is no escaping his presence. There is no such thing as being beyond the reach of his care. He is with you in every moment of your travail, because he lives inside you.

When you are sitting in the doctor's office, you've carried him there with you. In your moment of physical pain, he is right there with you. When a loved one has turned his back on you, he is still right there with you. When you've gotten devastating news, he is there with you. When you're distressed and confused, he is with you. No matter how hard and dark your situation, you are never alone, because you've carried him with you wherever you go and into whatever hard thing you're experiencing.

Your Lord, in all his power and glory, in the full expression of his mercy and grace and with your welfare in mind, is always with you because you are the place where he now lives. God's presence is not just your hope; it's your identity as a child of God. There's no better hope for a sufferer. All that God is, he is for us, because he lives inside us. He is near to you in your suffering; in fact, he couldn't be nearer, because you are the temple in which he resides. But there is more.

"I Will Not Leave You or Forsake You"

"I will not leave you or forsake you." This promise found in Joshua 1:5 is given numerous times in Scripture. Every time one of God's children or the whole community of God's children faced something hard, new, difficult, or overwhelming, God greeted them with this promise. He never called them to a task, sent them to a destination, or led them into difficulty and then abandoned them. No matter how hard the situation or inadequate their response, God was with them and for them. The declaration that he would never leave them is a significant reminder and protection for everyone who suffers.

First, these words are a humbling reminder that God remains faithful to us no matter what, not because of what is in us, but because of what's in him. If the consistency of my prayer or the faithfulness of my worship or the constancy of my obedience were what bought me his continued presence, he would have forsaken me long ago. I know it is true of me, and I'm sure it's true of you, that in moments of travail, I often fall way below God's standard. Sometimes confusion interrupts my prayer, or wonderment about what God is doing gets in the way of heartfelt worship. Sometimes I listen too much to the lies of the Enemy or feel too weak to do what God has commanded. Sometimes my heart is filled with more envy than gratitude, and my mouth speaks more complaint than praise. Sometimes I would rather have relief from pain than the sweetness of his presence. Sometimes I'm just mad that God has let such hard things enter my door. There are moments when I don't want to read his Word or hear songs of his goodness. Sometimes in my travail, I avoid the fellowship of his people. Sometimes I take my pain out on those around me.

My track record is far from perfect. I couldn't buy God's faithful presence with my performance. If I had to earn the right to have him stay with me, I would have no hope. Suffering exposes weaknesses, not just in a physical body or in our relationships but also in our hearts. Difficulty exposes weak joy, weak love, and fickle worship. Suffering reminds us that we are not as righteous as we've thought and not as faithful as we've confessed to be. Suffering brings you and me to the end of ourselves. It exposes and confronts us. It makes it harder and harder to hold on to the delusion of our righteousness. This is why it is so important to remember that God is faithful to us, not because we are righteous, but because he is. He continues to love us, not because we perfectly love him, but because his love for us remains perfect. He remains near, not because we've never thought of running away, but because he would never turn his back on the promises he's made to us. You didn't earn his faithful presence by your obedience, and your disobedience won't take it away. The central message of Scripture is that God is with us forever because of one thing and one thing alone: his grace!

In your suffering, with so many things to worry about, you don't have to waste your spiritual and emotional energy on the fear that you will be forsaken by the One who has the power to do for you what no one else can. He is in you, he is with you, he is for you, and he will never leave.

God's promise to never forsake us is not only a huge and comforting reminder as our sin and our suffering combine into a messy and embarrassing mix, but it's a significant spiritual protection as well. One of the most regular and devious attacks of the Enemy is exposed, by these words, as a lie that it is. Like the lion who chases the herd of deer to get them running and expose the weak ones, so Satan does his horrible work when and where we are weak. His lies have the power to deepen your desperation and weaken your resolve. They have the power to make you feel that you've been taken advantage of and duped. They have the power to make you wonder why you followed God in the first place, why you believed so many things you couldn't prove. Suffering makes us susceptible to the one voice we should never hear and that will always do us harm.

The central lie of Satan to all God's suffering children comes in the form of this question: "Where is your God now?" The lie embedded in this question is that our suffering is clear evidence that we have been forsaken by God. And if God would leave us to such travail, how is he worthy of our trust? It is a direct attack on the truthfulness and goodness of God. Satan is not so much mocking us for having believed as he is attacking the character of the One who has "tricked" us into believing by huge promises that our suffering now proves were never true. How horrible to rob suffering people of their only place to look for hope. Satan's question—"Where is your God now?"—doesn't expose God's untrustworthiness; it exposes the utter hatred of the Father of Lies.

God's often-repeated declaration that he will not leave sits on the pages of his Word as a protection against the lies to which suffering makes us susceptible. He has told you he will never leave so that when Satan tries to convince you that you have been forsaken, you will not listen. His words are a warning of temptations that every sufferer faces. His words are meant to ease your panic and erase your fear. When Satan tells you that God has turned his back on you, God's words are meant to remind you that he still holds you close and carries you near his heart.

With his here-forever presence comes his here-forever wisdom, his here-forever grace, his here-forever strength, his here-forever authority, his here-forever love, his here-forever mercy, his here-forever righteousness, and his here-forever patience. Everything in life ends or dies in some way. Nothing in this world remains the same forever. Many of the things we bank on end up failing us in the end. But God never will.

In an indescribable act of unmerited grace, he has made you the place where he lives, and in the faithfulness of that grace he will never walk away from you. In your suffering you will again and again fail to say or do the right thing. Under the weight of difficulty, you will lose your way for a while. You will drag yourself out of bed only to have a debilitating day of spiritual struggle. You will get very sad or very mad. One moment you will long for people to be with you and the next moment wish they would leave you alone. You won't always be comforted by the words of your loved ones, and there will be moments when you will wish they'd stop saying the things they say. Sometimes you will rest in God's rule, and other times you will be haunted by the future.

But in all the emotional and spiritual ups and downs, on the good days and the bad days, when you fight or succumb, one thing is for sure. Your Lord is with you, and there is no struggle without or war within that will ever drive him away. And his presence guarantees that in your suffering, you will have everything you need.

Review and Reflect

1. What are the benefits of preaching Scripture's truths to yourself when you are suffering? Which biblical truths help you the most?

2. Our culture defines *hope* differently from how the Bible defines it. Considering this chapter, how would you define *hope*?

3. Paul Tripp lists many statements about God's character. Which are most encouraging to you? Which had you not considered before now?

4. What are the daily implications of God promising to always be with you?

5. After finishing the chapter, how do you understand Paul Tripp's point that suffering can be a blessing and a joy?

Heart Reset

- Joshua 1:5

- Isaiah 40:1–31

- Matthew 28:20

11

The Comfort of God's Sovereignty

I didn't know that I could feel so out of control. I am a doer and a planner. I tend to have a project-oriented way of approaching life. I know exactly what I want to accomplish every day, how fast I need to work, and all that needs to be in place to finish my task. I tend to hate delay and chafe against interruptions. I am always aware of everything I need to control in order to get things done. And I know the people I need to support my efforts. You wouldn't generally characterize me as "controlling" in the negative sense of what that means, but you would surely see me as task oriented and maybe on my bad days a little too much of a self-sovereign.

Then I got sick. I want to take you back to those first moments that I wrote about in chapter 1. That first hour in the emergency ward examining room is a case study in loss of control. Suddenly things got very serious. Five physicians were poking, prodding, and pricking me from seemingly every direction. I was told that my questions couldn't be answered and that I wasn't going to leave the hospital anytime soon. Suddenly my life was in the hands of people I didn't know, my body was doing things it shouldn't do, and the rest of my life and ministry was on hold. As they wheeled me to a longer-term room, I was having trouble processing it all. Processing is what I do, helping people make sense of their lives from the perspective of the gospel of Jesus Christ. I wasn't processing; I was reeling. I was bombarded with so many questions that I was confused.

I could feel my life being yanked out of my order-loving hands. Then those horrible spasms started. My body shook and cramped, with accompanying spikes of intense pain, and I had no ability to turn it off. I never thought that I would be afraid of my own body, but I was. I was so out of control that everything else important to me faded into insignificance. All I could think of was surviving the physical trauma that had invaded my body. Just when the spasms began to subside, the doctors visited my room with dire descriptions of my diagnoses.

I kept asking the doctors when I would be released, but they evaded my question. I wanted to get back to my routine and my project-oriented lifestyle. Little did I know of the multiple surgeries, hospital stays, and months of convalescing that would become my life for a long time. Little did I know that I would never again be physically the same. I was in the throes of something I had no power to control, and other than doing what the doctors told me to do, there was nothing I could do about it.

Suffering Clarifies Who Is in Control

Hardship has the power to burst the bubble of our self-sovereignty. I don't think I'm alone in saying that I'm tempted to give myself comfort by convincing myself that I have more control over people, places, and things than I actually have. We want to believe that if we eat the right things and do the right exercises, we can control our health. We buy into thinking that if we parent our children well, we can guarantee that they will turn out all right. We want to believe that if we budget well, invest wisely, and save carefully, we can assure a good financial future. We want to think that if we dedicate ourselves to a loving marriage, we can secure its health and permanence. These are all good things to do, but the assumption that doing them controls outcomes is just not true.

From the very first breath of Adam, the Bible confronts our delusions of and desire for control. It is clear that Adam and Eve were not created for independent, self-sufficient living but for dependent, others-reliant living. And, like Adam and Eve, we don't have what it takes to make it well on our own because we don't have the power to supply all we need for this to be possible. Adam and Eve weren't made to make up their own rules and to live as they thought best. They were made to live inside the boundaries of the rules and purposes of someone greater. And they weren't placed in a world that would submit to their commands and do their bidding. They were called to be the resident managers of a world created and held together by the sovereign power of God.

Yes, we've been given many natural intellectual, emotional, and spiritual gifts, and if we exercise them as God intended, we can do much to help our lives be relatively comfortable and stable. But we can't take credit or blame for things we had no power to produce. If I were in control, there is no way I would have allowed physical travail into my life. In fact, I will make a confession. If I were in control, I wouldn't let difficulty of any kind, big or small, into my life. Hardship confronts us with our tendency to assume that we're in greater control than we really are, and because we think we are, we take way more credit for the good things in our lives than we should. The opposite is true as well. Because we assume greater control than we actually have, we blame ourselves for things we have no power to cause. A loving wife of an unfaithful husband haunts herself with questions about what she could have done to keep him from wandering. Good parents blame themselves for the spiritual and relational rebellion of their children. People who have invested with untrustworthy investors kick themselves for being so trusting. Even children tend to find reasons to blame themselves for the separation of their parents. In all these cases, people are adding to their suffering by assuming power and control that they didn't have and never will have.

Suffering causes us to scan our lives and face the fact that we control very little. So we mourn not only our suffering but also what it has forced us to admit about ourselves. Our loss of the illusion of control also adds to the fear that accompanies suffering.

But realizing we are not in control is also one of suffering's biggest blessings. It's one of difficulty's paradoxical comforts. The fear and pain of being out of control stand before us as doorways to something very good. It's only when we give up the delusion that we've been or can be in greater control that we can find rest in the One who is in control in our place. Suffering proves that helplessness is the portal to help. It is only when we abandon our independence that we find rest in one greater. Hopelessness is the only doorway to hope. When we forsake our trust in our power, we're then ready to entrust ourselves to the power of another. Our smallness and weakness aren't our greatest dangers; the greatest danger is the delusion that we are bigger and stronger than we are or ever will be. Here is suffering's paradox: the very things we would do anything to avoid, the very things that confront our understanding of who we are, and the very things that cause us the most pain become the very things that usher into our lives the blessings of the help, hope, peace, and rest that we all long to experience.

I want to examine one more thing before I unpack the comforts every sufferer can find in God's sovereign control of all things. I want you to think with me about mystery. God does things that will remain a mystery. God brings into our lives life things that confuse us. At times we struggle to reconcile what God has said with what he's done. Sometimes God's declaration of who he is seems to contradict what he has ordained. Sometimes God's plan doesn't make sense. At times God appears bad, even though he tells us he is good. At times it is hard to live in the tension of what God has promised and what he has brought our way. There are passages in life when we live with more mystery than clarity. We all face times when we cry out for answers that we'll never get but that seem impossible to live without. Painful times come when we cry, "Why?" "If only ____," or "How long?"

Everyone faces moments when a cloud of mystery covers theological clarity. In these moments we don't want a theological outline or a set of wisdom principles. We cry out for an answer that will dispel the mystery that has us in its emotional and spiritual hold. At times we are tempted to withhold our trust until God gives an explanation. There are times when we're tempted to believe that we won't be able to trust until we are able to understand, that our peace of heart is dependent on mysteries being solved.

Here's the problem. God's secret will is called his "secret will" because it's secret. In his Word God graciously defines his character, and unfolds his grand redemptive plan, but he doesn't explain himself when it comes to the details of how and why he rules his world the way he does. This means that embracing the truth of his sovereignty doesn't remove the confusion of mystery from our lives. So rest and peace of heart will never be found in understanding what God has ordained for us and his world, because we'll always lack understanding to some degree. God knows that we are incapable of carrying the burden of sovereign knowledge that he carries, so he lovingly protects us by telling us what we need to know: we are to rest in him and live as he has ordained, while he protects us from what would overwhelm us.

When our children were young and I had to say no to something they wanted, they would say, "Daddy, why? Why?" I knew that they wouldn't be able to understand my reasons, so I would say, "Daddy would love to tell you why, but you would not understand. You can get mad at Daddy and say, 'My daddy is a bad daddy because he says no to me,' or you can say, 'I don't know why my daddy said no to me, but I know my daddy is a good daddy who loves me.'" Then I would say, "Trust your daddy. I really do want what's best for you." Because we don't understand, and because things around us or near us don't always seem good, it is tempting to question the wisdom, love, and goodness of God. It is tempting to let our situational confusion begin to sow seeds of doubt, leading us to question truths that the Bible makes clear and that we have held dear.

When Job, who had lost everything, asked God for a reason for his suffering, seeking answers that we all tend to cry out for in the devastation of hardship, God didn't give him answers. Stop and read Job 38–41 and then consider Job's response. Rather than giving Job answers he wouldn't understand and that his heart couldn't contain, God answered Job by pointing to himself, to his presence, power, and glory. He knew that Job's instinct was to seek answers, when what Job really needed was to seek God. Nothing good ever comes when a sufferer withholds trust in God because he's unable to understand why something bad has happened. Yet there are moments when I am tempted, and you will be tempted, to do just that.

So where do we run with our questions? What do we do with our lack of answers? It never works to demand what you'll never have. It never works to require of God what he, in his love and wisdom, knows it's best not to give. So the rest of heart that every sufferer longs for never comes from demanding understanding.

Rest comes from putting your trust in the One who understands and rules all the things that confuse you. God is never caught up short. He never has a second of confusion. He never regrets what he's done. He is never confused as to what to do. He has no quandaries, and he never lives with unsolved mysteries. He rules all things, he knows all things, and there is nothing that he doesn't understand.

But there's more. The One who rules and understands everything is the definition of all that is right, true, faithful, loving, powerful, and gracious. His rule is always good because he is good. So it's very important to not allow the confusion of suffering to redefine for you who God is. Rather, we all need to accept the limits of our understanding, while we let God's declaration of who he is in Scripture define the hope we can have, because he is with us in our suffering and rules all the details of it. Hope is found not in trying to solve all the mysteries that suffering brings our way but in running into the arms of the One who has no mystery and offers us his presence, power, and promises.

Understanding the Comfort Found in God's Rule

> For his dominion is an everlasting dominion,
>> and his kingdom endures from generation to generation;
> all the inhabitants of the earth are accounted as nothing,
>> and he does according to his will among the host of
>> heaven
>> and among the inhabitants of the earth;
> and none can stay his hand
>> or say to him, "What have you done?" (Dan. 4:34b–35)

I love these words spoken by Nebuchadnezzar, a powerful ruler in ancient Babylon, after he'd been humbled by the hand of God. These are words of humble surrender and also of glorious hope for anyone struggling through the hardships and disappointments of life. May these words be written on our hearts and give hope to us when nothing else in life can. I want to use these words as a backdrop for unpacking the practical, life-giving hope that God's sovereign rule offers to every one of his suffering children.

1. God's Rule Stretches from before Origins to beyond Destiny

It's hard to stretch our imagination far enough to grasp that there never was nor will there ever be a moment in the history of the universe that is out of control. God ruled from his throne before the universe was created and set in motion; God sits on his throne right now, and he'll continue to rule after the world as we know it has passed away. It may not look like it, you may not understand it, and you may quarrel with how he does it, but every second of the past, present, and future passes under his careful rule.

This is practical and hope giving for all of us because every second of our lives, from conception to final destiny, is under his sovereign management. Yes, we face things we never thought we'd face, and, yes, many of those things are very hard. No, we can't always discern why God makes the choices that he, in his infinite wisdom, makes, but we shouldn't allow hardship to lead us to conclude that something has gotten in the way of his rule. As Nebuchadnezzar rightly states, nothing in heaven or on earth can stop his rule or force him to give account for it.

His words paint a huge contrast between God and us, and we need to let that sink in. I can't even keep control of my car keys, let alone the things that give shape and direction to my life. But that shouldn't cause me to conclude that these things are out of control, because they are under God's control. His will is always done. His plan always succeeds. Everything in creation does his bidding. And he's infinitely wise and perfectly good. We shouldn't interpret suffering as evidence of his absence, weakness, distance, or lack of care.

This means that there's never a moment when I can't go for help, and there's never a moment when God is incapable of helping me, because he rules everything that needs to be ruled so that he can give me the help that I need. *Have you let suffering weaken your belief in the moment-by-moment rule of your Lord?*

2. God's Rule Is Global

When we go into a new location, a different situation, or a new community of people, we often experience anxiety. This natural anxiety is the result of the limits of our understanding and personal power when we enter a place we don't yet know or an experience we've never had. No wonder our minds race and our hearts beat a little faster. We wonder what we'll have to face, how we'll be treated, and whether we'll make it through.

Such is the experience of anyone who has ever suffered the unexpected. I had never been seriously sick; I had never endured a long hospital stay; I had never been too sick to do what God called me to do; I had never experienced intolerable pain; I had never endured failing, damaged kidneys; I had never had to face surgery after surgery; and I had never had to face the fact that I will bear significant physical weakness until I die. No wonder I was assaulted with grief and fear. No wonder I was a bit paralyzed by the impossibility of it all. No wonder.

It's here that God's global sovereignty is so precious. Your story will take you places you never thought you'd be. Your life will travel roads you don't feel ready to travel. You'll end in places far from what you would have chosen. There will be situations in which you wonder how in the world you got there. Wherever your story takes you, you'll never arrive there first, because your Lord is already there in sovereign presence and power, and he rules that place in infinite wisdom and holiness. He has the power to do what he wills, and the way he rules is always right.

David captures this well with these familiar words from Psalm 139:

> Where shall I go from your Spirit?
>> Or where shall I flee from your presence?
> If I ascend to heaven, you are there!
>> If I make my bed in Sheol, you are there!
> If I take the wings of the morning
>> and dwell in the uttermost parts of the sea,
> even there your hand shall lead me,
>> and your right hand shall hold me. (vv. 7–10)

Could it be that you've forgotten that the hard place you're in right now is ruled by your Lord of wisdom, power, and grace?

3. God's Rule Is Individual and Detailed

One of my all-time favorite Bible passages is Acts 17:26–27, which says that God "made from one man every nation of mankind to live on all the face of the earth, having determined allotted periods and the boundaries of their dwelling place, that they should seek God, and perhaps feel their way toward him and find him. Yet he is actually not far from each one of us." I don't know if I can give justice to the amazing reality that these verses capture, but I will try. When you think of God's sovereignty, you shouldn't mentally picture God on a throne somewhere off in the distant heavens organizing the big events of the universe. The picture Paul gives in Acts couldn't be more different.

Paul wants us to know that God's sovereignty is gloriously more than a "big event" rule. He wants us to know that God cares about and is involved with the details of our lives, and Paul gives us specific examples. He says that God determines our "allotted periods" and the "boundaries of [our] dwelling place." You may read that and think, "What in the world is he talking about?" When Paul talks about "allotted periods," he means the length of your life, and when he says, "boundaries of their dwelling place," he means the address where we live. Think of God as directly involved with the length of the life of everyone who has ever lived and the exact address of everyone who has ever walked the face of the earth! He is just that present and powerful!

But there is more here. God has chosen to rule this way to be near to each one of us. Sure, Paul believes in God's *transcendent* sovereignty, the fact that he exists above all, but here he is teaching the truth of God's *immanent* sovereignty, his nearness. Paul want us to know this because wherever we are, whatever we are going through, God is so near that we can reach out and touch him. He is sovereignly close. He is reachable, touchable, in your time of need. The God who is your hope in suffering is near because he has been and will ever be involved with even the little details of your life. His sovereignty guarantees that God is reachable in those moments when you think there is no helper who can reach you with what you need. *Are you in the habit of telling yourself that God's rule promises that he is always near?*

4. God's Rule Is an Expression of His Character

God's sovereignty would not be such a huge comfort were it not for the fact that his rule is an expression of his glory. His rule is an expression, not a contradiction, of his love. His rule is an expression, not a compromise, of his wisdom. His rule never betrays his grace. His rule is an extension of his justice. His rule pictures his holiness. He rules in mercy. His sovereignty is tempered, directed, and expressed by his character. Because of this, in all your pain and confusion you can rest assured that the One who rules over every hard thing you experience is trustworthy because he is perfectly holy, lovingly wise, and good in every way. *When you are confused by God's rule, do you remind yourself of his character?*

5. God Rules for Our Benefit

At the end of Ephesians 1 Paul assures his readers that God not only rules but he rules all things for their sake. He says that Jesus now rules over everything for the sake of the church. Let this sink in for a minute. In amazing grace God has chosen to expend his power and authority in a way that directly benefits his children. You and I may not understand it or think that we are experiencing it, but God's rule is benevolent and redemptive. He does what he does not just for his own glory but also for the glory of his children. His sovereignty has you and me in view. As he rules, he remembers us. He remembers every promise he has made, what we need, what we are going through, the broken, groaning world he's left us in, and what it's like to walk in our shoes. The One in charge of it all is for us and exercises that authority for our benefit. *Do you remind yourself that the One who rules everything, rules it all for your good?*

Yes, we all live in moments, locations, situations, or relationships that seem to be spinning out of control, but they are not out of control. Yes, they are way beyond the scope of our control, but they under the rule of One who is not only in complete control but is also perfectly good in every way. By the grace of the life, death, and resurrection of Jesus, God is your Father. He exercises his sovereignty with a father's love for you. He hears your cries for help, and he stays near, and he is always reachable. He has authority you will never have, and he exercises it with a wise and loving heart for your benefit and the benefit of each of his children.

Review and Reflect

1. How has suffering forced you to acknowledge that you aren't in control?

2. What about the mystery of God tends to frustrate you? What about it do you find comforting?

3. Job in his suffering questioned God, but God simply pointed to himself rather than answer Job's questions. Why? Where do you see God's care in this response?

4. In your suffering, how have you allowed yourself to forget God's constant presence, rule, and character?

5. Paul Tripp reminds us that God in his goodness rules over all things for our good. How does this encourage you, and where have you seen it in your life?

Heart Reset
- Job 38:1–42:6

- Acts 17:26–27

- Ephesians 1:15–23

12

The Comfort of God's Purpose

They're the universal cries of sufferers everywhere. They come out of you spontaneously, needing no conscious thought. They assault your peace and diminish your hope. The questions haunt you late at night and interrupt your sleep and are the unwanted friend that greets you in the morning. Sometimes these cries are mixed with anger, sometimes with fear, but always colored by the pain of facing the unwanted and the unexpected. Your theology might not keep these cries coming from deep within your heart. Sometimes you seek some kind of answer; other times you don't really expect the relief that an answer would provide.

"Why? Why me? Why now?" These are the questions that come out of us as we deal with the seeming spontaneity, irrationality, unpredictability, and purposelessness of suffering. On the surface suffering doesn't seem good; it seems to attack what's good and like it will leave us with nothing good. Suffering seems to be a horrible, unnecessary interruption. It feels as if a thief has just beaten you up and robbed you of precious belongings—you know you'll never be the same again. Suffering robs you of the illusion of control, and it has the power to pick your pockets clean. It causes you to hope that the day will be over, while you dread the day to come. It throws you into an alien world you never wanted to traverse. No wonder you cry, "Why?"

I could see my life unfolding before me. I thought I knew what God was doing. Life and ministry were as good and as fruitful as they'd ever been. I was flooded with wonderful things to do and a seemingly endless catalog of opportunities. I loved getting up in the morning. I loved the fact that, by God's grace, every day I invested my gifts in things of eternal significance. I was surrounded and supported by a team of smart people who cared not only about the ministry to which we together had been called but also about me. It seemed that God was in it and honored by it, and it made sense that he would keep it going forever. Why would God ever mess with something that worked to give him glory and convinced people to live in rest and submission to him? Why would he not do anything he could to keep me strong, active, and speaking for him? Why would he not give me a greater voice to point people to him? Why?

I thought I knew the plan until I took that fateful walk to Jefferson Hospital on that fall afternoon in 2014. In one moment, in that emergency room, the seemingly purposeful collided with the seemingly purposeless. God not only interrupted what seemed to be his plan for me but left me so damaged that I would never again be able to do ministry as I once had. Why would he give me these gifts and opportunities but leave me too weak to use them? I did lie in the pain of those first few days in the hospital and silently cry, "Why? Why me? Why now?" My suffering has been not just physical but deeply theological. And yours is too.

You may not consciously try to push your suffering through the grid of your beliefs, but your cries and questions are richly theological. Like me, you would love to make a personal appointment with God, sit down with him in his celestial office, and have him respond personally and directly to your questions. Or maybe what you're enduring has made you wonder if distant, impersonal forces in nature have more to do with the unfolding of your story than you'd previously thought. For sure, like me, your suffering has drawn out of you profoundly important questions that you long to have answered.

Does My Suffering Have a Purpose?

Let me cut to the chase here. The biblical answer is yes, your suffering has a purpose. No other answer does justice to what the Bible says about who God is and how our world is ordered. Yes, at street level you may experience chaos and confusion, and, no, God won't make the details of his purposes known to you, but there's tremendous comfort in the definitive answer of Scripture to the question every sufferer asks.

Maybe it seems more comforting to be able to separate God from your hardship and the pain of it, but there's no real peace of heart to be found that way. Perhaps you're tempted to tell yourself that the cause of your suffering is merely the normal breakdown of the natural laws of the universe and God has nothing to do with it. But would it actually give you peace to know that God, with all his power, stands idly by as his broken creation brings devastation into your life? Would it be comforting to think that there is no one to cry out to for help because there's no person in charge of what you're facing? Or would you find comfort in telling yourself that all the bad things in life come from Satan's hands? Would it be comforting to believe that he has the power to interrupt God's good plan for you? Would it give you hope to think that the person in charge of your suffering has no interest in hearing your cries for help but rather finds delight in your travail?

It really is hard to grasp, but real hope and comfort are found only in those words spoken by Nebuchadnezzar after he had been humbled by God:

At the end of the days I, Nebuchadnezzar, lifted my eyes to heaven, and my reason returned to me, and I blessed the Most High, and praised and honored him who lives forever,

> For his dominion is an everlasting dominion,
>> and his kingdom endures from generation to
>> generation;
> all the inhabitants of the earth are accounted as
>> nothing,
>> and he does according to his will among the host of
>> heaven
>> and among the inhabitants of the earth;
> and none can stay his hand
>> or say to him, "What have you done?"
> (Dan. 4:34–35)

Even Nebuchadnezzar's expansive words don't fully express the glory of God and the extent of his power and authority. Scripture makes very clear that God is in absolute control of the world that he created and the lives of the people he has placed in it. We don't live under the dictates of impersonal scientific forces. We don't live under the sovereign control of the forces of evil. We live in a world that's been terribly broken by sin but still sits under the power and authority of the One who created it. You may not see his hand, and it may be very hard to accept that what you've had to endure has come under God's watch, but Scripture is clear about the nature and extent of his rule. The fact that God is in control tells us that there's divine reason and purpose to all we face.

You may say, "But, Paul, where is the comfort in this?" First, even though we endure things that don't seem to be good, there is comfort in knowing that the One in charge of all that happens is holy, righteous, good, wise, and loving in every way. He is the ultimate definition of all these attributes. He is also tender, patient, and kind. God is never malevolent, unjust, uncaring, duplicitous, or devious. He's after the ultimate good for his creation, and for us who bear his image, he's moving creation to the moment when he will finally make all things new.

If God had nothing whatsoever to do with what we're facing, he would have little ability to come to our aid. Because God is intimately involved with everything we face, he is also preeminently able to offer just the kind of help we all need in our moment of hardship.

But there's another thing to think about here. When God's children are suffering, they tend to cling to his promises more tightly. As God's children, we pin our security to the hope that God will actually do for us what his promises tell us he'll do. We hold onto this hope, even though we're unable to see his hand or figure out how he'll break through our hardship to deliver anything good. It's important to understand, as we are holding tightly to God's promises, that our hope depends entirely on his sovereign rule. A person has the ability to ensure he can do what he's promised only in situations he controls. When my children were home I could make good on my promises to them, because I was in charge of the location where those promises needed to be delivered. In the same way, the reliability of God's promises to us is dependent on his rule over the situations where they're needed.

The One in control has incalculable power and unobstructed authority, and he is the definition of love, which is very good news to his suffering children.

So, If God Has a Purpose for Our Suffering, What Is It?

Even though the Bible doesn't answer your specific *why* questions—the kind of questions every sufferer asks—it does unveil why God allows hardship into the lives of his children. There is tremendous comfort in the purpose of God revealed in Scripture.

God lovingly clues us into his purpose so that in the middle of our suffering we have reason to hope.

1. We Suffer Because We Live in a Fallen World
(2 Cor. 4:7–10)

You may be thinking, "Where is the comfort in knowing that we live in a fallen world?" It is comforting because it means that the painful things we deal with are not some bad accident, horrible luck, or indication of a massive failure of God's plan. If any of these things were true, we would have reason to feel powerless and hopeless. Note how the Bible talks about our experience in the here and now:

> We have this treasure in jars of clay, to show that the sur-passing power belongs to God and not to us. We are afflicted in every way, but not crushed; perplexed, but not driven to despair; persecuted, but not forsaken; struck down, but not destroyed; always carrying in the body the death of Jesus, so that the life of Jesus may also be manifested in our bodies. (2 Cor. 4:7–10)

No place in Scripture treats the fact of our suffering with shock, surprise, frustration, or dismay. Rather, suffering is pre-sented to us as the normal experience of everyone living between the fall of Adam and Eve and the future coming of Christ. God hasn't failed, his plan hasn't failed, and you and I haven't been abandoned. And because we know that God has a purpose for leaving us for a period of time in a terribly broken world, we can suffer but not be hauntingly perplexed or in constant despair, nor feel forsaken or that we're about to be destroyed. Hope for sufferers is rooted in the fact that they've not been singled out or forsaken but that what is painful has a purpose. If suffering has a purpose, then there is reason to believe that good things will come out of what doesn't seem good.

The picture in 2 Corinthians 4 is of cracked clay vessels, but you can see treasure shining through the cracks. Wow! There's a whole lot of content in that little word picture. First, it reminds us that we were never unbreakable steel vessels and that we weren't created to be independently strong. We were created to be fragile, because God wants to accomplish something good through our fragility. He allows us to be cracked so we will finally get the fact that hope and security are never found by what's in us but only by what's in him. In order to accomplish this, he has to put us in situations where we can't make it on the basis of our strength and wisdom but instinctively reach out for help instead.

The picture of cracked vessels with treasure shining through the cracks is a picture of being filled. Suffering causes us to really know who we are and who God is and to begin to really celebrate what we've been given. God doesn't always fill your cracks but often uses your cracks to fill you up with a sense of his presence, grace, and glory.

God leaves us in this broken world because what it produces in us is way better than the comfortable life we all want. I haven't always felt this way, but it's true that in our suffering God isn't saddling us with less but graciously giving us more. This is why we can endure hardship without feeling forsaken or giving way to despair. *Has suffering robbed you of your hope? Has it tempted you to tell yourself that you've been forsaken?*

2. We Suffer Because God Uses It to Produce Good in Us (James 1:2–4)

The comfort in James 1:2–4 confronts us with what we truly want out of life. There are only two types of motivating hopes. You either hook your hope to a physical, situational life of comfort, success, strength, and pleasure or to a life of rich spiritual awakening, growth, and Godward glory. The Bible presents the second option as not only infinitely more satisfying in the long run but also that for which we were made. Because we were made for it, it does a much better job of satisfying the longing that's in all our hearts. Suffering in the hands of God is a powerful tool of personal growth and transformation. Here's what God does in us through the tool of hardship:

> Count it all joy, my brothers, when you meet trials of various kinds, for you know that the testing of your faith produces steadfastness. And let steadfastness have its full effect, that you may be perfect and complete, lacking in nothing. (James 1:2–4)

That is a remarkable passage because it calls and alerts us to something counterintuitive. We don't typically experience joy in suffering; in fact, many of us lose our joy even in the face of the smallest obstacles. Now, don't misunderstand what James is calling you to here. He's not saying you should rejoice because of pain and loss. This is not a call to some kind of joyful Christian stoicism. Rather, James is saying that you have reason to rejoice in the middle of your travail because of how God is using your suffering to produce in you what you could never produce in yourself. Suffering in the hands of God is used to fill you up, to grow you up, and to complete God's work in you.

James is saying that the bad things you endure are a tool of a very good thing that God is doing in you and for you. So in the very moment when you and I think we've been forsaken, we're actually being graced with God's rescuing, transforming, and delivering power. And what is it that we're being delivered from? James's answer is clear: we are being delivered from ourselves. It is humbling to admit that the greatest disaster in our lives is not what we suffer, but the sin inside us, which separates us from God and always leads to death. While we tend to be intolerant of hardship and difficulty, God is intolerant of our sin, so he uses hard things to deliver us from it. The only name for this is grace. It's true that grace often comes in uncomfortable forms. When we cry out for grace, we're often already getting it, but it's not the grace of release; it's the grace of rescue and transformation, because that's the grace we really need.

In our suffering God is at work to give us something much better than what we want. He's not content to dispense temporary relief, when eternal change is what we really need. In the zeal of redeeming love, he uses hard tools to produce soft but sturdy hearts, and that's a very good thing. Think of the power in suffering to change us:

- *Suffering has the power to destroy our self-reliance.* We weren't created to be self-reliant, so self-reliance never produces good things in us. We were created to be dependent on God and mutually dependent on one another. Our lives are a community project. Suffering exposes the fact that we're not self-sufficient, that we do, in fact, need others. The pain and weakness of suffering cause us to cry out to God, perhaps more genuinely, more deeply, and more humbly than ever before.

- *Suffering has the power to expose our self-righteousness.* We like to tell ourselves that we're spiritually okay, but suffering also exposes the bad things that still live inside us. In our pain we're irritable, envious, demanding, impatient, doubtful, and angry. Suffering doesn't make us this way, but it draws out what's been inside us already. Suffering demonstrates that we're not grace graduates, that there's still sin inside us, and that we desperately need the Savior's grace. What comes out of us as we suffer proves that we need something profoundly more important than relief from situational, physical, relational, or cultural hardship.

- *Suffering has the power to lay waste to our idols.* Suffering has a way of exposing what's really dear to us, what we feel we can't live without, and what truly rules our hearts. It's not just that what we're going through is painful, but also that we've lost what was giving us value and worth. Suffering exposes the inadequacy of hooking our hope to the temporary treasures of the created world and positions our heart to hook our hope to the Creator in ways we've never done before.

Are you looking gratefully for the ways that God will use what's very hard to produce what's very good in you?

3. Suffering Prepares Us for How God Will Use Us (2 Cor. 1:3–9)

Here's the bottom line. If you're God's child, you've been liberated from the self-centered burden of living for yourself, and you've been freed to live for him. That means you've been called to be part of what God is doing in the lives of those around you and around the world. Ministry is not so much a career or a kind of episodic volunteerism; for every believer it's a lifestyle we've been called to. The problem is that we don't naturally have the desire to make personal sacrifices for the sake of ministry to others, and we need training. God uses suffering to make us both willing and ready to be part of what he's doing in the lives of others. No passage captures this better than 2 Corinthians 1:3–9:

> Blessed be the God and Father of our Lord Jesus Christ, the Father of mercies and God of all comfort, who comforts us in all our affliction, so that we may be able to comfort those who are in any affliction, with the comfort with which we ourselves are comforted by God. For as we share abundantly in Christ's sufferings, so through Christ we share abundantly in comfort too. If we are afflicted, it is for your comfort and

salvation; and if we are comforted, it is for your comfort, which you experience when you patiently endure the same sufferings that we suffer. Our hope for you is unshaken, for we know that as you share in our sufferings, you will also share in our comfort.

For we do not want you to be unaware, brothers, of the affliction we experienced in Asia. For we were so utterly burdened beyond our strength that we despaired of life itself. Indeed, we felt that we had received the sentence of death. But that was to make us rely not on ourselves but on God who raises the dead.

God causes us to long for and experience his comfort so that we would be ready to be agents of his comfort in the lives of others. This means that our suffering has ministry in view. Your hardships qualify you to be part of the most wonderful and important work in the universe.

I don't know about you, but I'm not always sympathetic and compassionate. I'm not always tender and generous in the face of the trials of others. But God has used my weakness, confusion, and fear to soften my heart and make me much more willing and able to enter into the trials of others with an understanding and compassionate heart. We all know that we don't own the blessings in our lives, that we are meant to pass them forward into the lives of others, but this passage confronts us with the fact that even our sufferings belong to the Lord for his use. Suffering is meant not to drive us inside ourselves but to lead us out to offer to others the beautiful hope, comfort, joy, and security that God has given us.

Notice how this passage ends. Like Paul, God will give us stories to tell, stories of how God met us in our darkest moments of panic and doom. He gives us stories to tell about how he lifts us up, gives us hope, brings peace to our hearts, and meets our needs. We tell others our stories not to point to us, but to point to God so that those to whom we minister will find their comfort in him too. *Where has God given you stories of suffering and comfort so that you can bring comfort to those around you who are suffering?*

4. Suffering Teaches Us That This World Is Not Our Final Home (2 Cor. 4:16–5:5)

Pay careful attention to the following passage:

> So we do not lose heart. Though our outer self is wasting away, our inner self is being renewed day by day. For this light momentary affliction is preparing for us an eternal weight of glory beyond all comparison, as we look not to the things that are seen but to the things that are unseen. For the things that are seen are transient, but the things that are unseen are eternal.
>
> For we know that if the tent that is our earthly home is destroyed, we have a building from God, a house not made with hands, eternal in the heavens. For in this tent we groan, longing to put on our heavenly dwelling, if indeed by putting it on we may not be found naked. For while we are still in this tent, we groan, being burdened—not that we would be unclothed, but that we would be further clothed, so that what is mortal may be swallowed up by life. He who has prepared us for this very thing is God, who has given us the Spirit as a guarantee. (2 Cor. 4:16–5:5)

This passage is all about spiritual preparation. As I've mentioned throughout this book, it's important to understand that this world isn't your final destination. When you live with a here-and-now mentality, you want this life to be as comfortable, predictable, pleasurable, successful, and enjoyable as it can be. Like the old commercial said, "You only go around once in life: Go for all the gusto you can." But the Bible is very clear that this is not all we have. It's clear that what God is doing in the here and now is working to prepare us for the final destination.

We're all like pilgrims on a great spiritual journey, living in the uncomfortable world of tents and temporary locations. All the hardship and loss we face are designed by God to prepare us for our eternal home. God is working through hardship to pry open our hands and loosen our hearts from our tight grip on the here and now. He's working to release us from the hope that this present world will ever be the paradise that our hearts long for. He's employing suffering to produce in our hearts a deep and motivating longing for a much, much better home, the eternal home that's the promise of his grace to us all. And he's given us his Spirit right now as the all-access pass to that home. Like a ticket that guarantees entrance, we carry the Spirit around with us to remind us that there's a home waiting for us where we'll be welcomed and taken in forever.

What we suffer isn't a failure of God's plan but a tool to bring us in line with God's plan so that we'll love what he's prepared for us more than we love our present comfort. *Where is there evidence in your life that you've been living with a destination mentality?*

So your suffering isn't purposeless, impersonal pain that robs you of what's good. It's a tool picked up by a Savior of wisdom, love, and grace to produce wonderful things in and through you that you could never produce on your own. In your pain he proves that he's near and working to take what's discouragingly painful and intolerably hard and produce out of it a harvest of good things. He works so that your faith and hope will blossom, your character will change and mature, and your willingness and ability to minister to others will increase. He isn't emptying you of good things but using hardship to fill you with the good things that only his grace can produce.

So you can say with hope and joy, even while you acknowledge the pain of suffering and loss, "Yes, there is purpose in my suffering, because God takes it as a tool in his hands to do things in and through me, things that are profoundly valuable and eternally good—so good that he's willing to take me to hard places to deliver these treasures." In your suffering, run, run, run to the comfort of God's purpose. If you do, day after day you'll be glad you did.

Review and Reflect

1. Why is it comforting to know that we live in a fallen world?

2. Have you ever considered that God's work is to deliver you from yourself? What does that look like in your daily life?

3. Paul Tripp writes that God "uses hard tools to produce soft but sturdy hearts" (p. 181). How have you seen that in his care for you?

4. In what ways have you seen God use the power of suffering to deliver you from your idols?

5. How has God used suffering to prepare you to serve him?

Heart Reset

- Daniel 4:34–35

- 2 Corinthians 1:3–9; 4:7–10

13

The Comfort of God's People

As I write this chapter I'm in the throes of an irony—or maybe not. Just as I began to stabilize physically and to learn to live with the physical deficits I've been left with, I have been hit with a virulent attack of shingles. Because of my dysfunctional immune system, the virus will be with me longer and the deep nerve pain will be more powerful than in more typical cases. I have been warned that the debilitating back pain I'm dealing with could be permanent. The physical travail of the last few days has been so severe that I have been unable to sleep or write or sit, nor am I comfortable lying down; I feel some relief only when standing. Pain medication gives some relief, but pain is still always with me.

On one hand, it's ironic that as I'm coming to the end of this book on suffering, I'm now dealing with yet another layer of it. It's tempting to be absorbed in all the *why* questions we tend to ask. It's tempting to wallow in self-pity. It's so tempting to be envious of friends who seem to have it so easy. It's tempting to give way to "how long" and "what next" fears. It's tempting to wonder if God really does hear my cries for help. Once again I'm confronted with the reality that suffering is not just physically, situationally, and relationally hard; it's also a moment-by-moment spiritual war. It's vital that I be aware of the dangers of this battle. But I'm reminded also that I'm not meant to fight this battle alone.

Suffering powerfully highlights what has always been true—we were not created for independent living. Suffering exposes our weakness, our blindness, and our lack of control. Suffering preaches that our lives are a community project. Suffering reminds us that God's grace doesn't work to propel our independence but to deepen our vertical and horizontal dependence. The strong, independent, self-made person is a delusion. Everyone needs help and assistance. Everyone has learned at the feet of someone else. Everyone is strengthened by others. To fight community, to quest for self-sufficiency, is not only a denial of your spiritual need; it's a denial of your humanity. Suffering is a messenger telling us that to be human is to be dependent.

So perhaps I'm not in the middle of an irony but of a very wise plan. As I sit to write a chapter about the comfort of the community of faith, God works to put me in grave need of the very thing that I'm writing about. Clearly God has called me to experience what I had no plan or desire to experience in order to produce in me what I could never create on my own. The Bible has a name for this: *grace*. I've not been forgotten, I'm not being messed with, and this is profoundly more than another round of bad luck. What I'm experiencing is the very uncomfortable grace that I have written and spoken so much about. This physical travail, in the hands of my Savior, is a tool used to drive me away from self-sufficiency and into a deeper dependency on God and his people.

I've cried out to and been held up by a circle of faithful brothers and sisters. I can't imagine how different this hardship would be if I'd had to walk through it alone. One of God's sweetest gifts to us between the "already" of our conversion and the "not yet" of our homegoing is the gift of the body of Christ. God makes his invisible grace visible by sending people of grace to give grace to people who need grace. His people are meant to be the look on his face, the touch of his hand, the sound of his voice, the evidence of his love, the picture of his presence, and the visible demonstration of his faithfulness. God hasn't left us to ourselves but has blessed us with an abundant community of help. The question is whether your suffering will drive you inward to go it alone or call you outward in humble, honest, and willing dependency.

There's a wonderful example of humble dependency in 2 Corinthians 1:

> We do not want you to be unaware, brothers, of the affliction we experienced in Asia. For we were so utterly burdened beyond our strength that we despaired of life itself. Indeed, we felt that we had received the sentence of death. But that was to make us rely not on ourselves but on God who raises the dead. He delivered us from such a deadly peril, and he will deliver us. On him we have set our hope that he will deliver us again. You also must help us by prayer, so that many will give thanks on our behalf for the blessing granted us through the prayers of many. (vv. 8–11)

Each time I read these verses I'm impressed with the shocking honesty of the apostle Paul. He was a powerfully influential man of faith, one you wouldn't expect to be going through the struggle of heart that these verses portray. These words blow the lid off any image we might have of Paul as an independently spiritual man who lived way above the spiritual battles that are common to us all. This icon of gospel clarity, this messenger of gospel hope, this missionary to the hopeless, desperately needs for himself all that he holds out to others. So in the context of one troublesome event, he humbly unzips his heart and reveals the unsettling conflict that lives there.

Notice that Paul doesn't tell us the exact situation; this is not a detailed report of his difficulty. Paul's focus is the impact that this situation had on him and those with him. He is candidly confessing a deep spiritual struggle. He is confessing to where his thoughts went and what his heart experienced. This is more of a humble appeal for help than a careful communication of what he's suffering. We tend to enjoy telling people in detail about the thing we're suffering, while we tend to be more guarded about how we're suffering. Celebrating the gift of the body of Christ in the middle of suffering isn't about reporting suffering but about confessing the struggle in the midst of it. It isn't just about communicating what you're going through but also being honest about how you're going through it.

Let's examine what Paul says. First, he admits to weakness, saying, "We were so utterly burdened beyond our strength." He doesn't hide behind spiritual platitudes. He doesn't act as if he's something that he's not. He has no fear of publicly communicating his frailty. But what he says next is key. It's the thing that many sufferers seem afraid of doing, and because they are, they don't receive the kind of comforting care that God has provided through his people. Paul confesses to the despair of heart he experienced as he was faced with his weakness and inability. These words, "We despaired of life itself. Indeed, we felt . . . the sentence of death," capture the spiritual battle in Paul's heart that was underneath the physical travail. Remember, this is the apostle Paul. No figure looms larger in the New Testament except Jesus, yet here he is, thinking, "This is it. I simply don't have what it takes to make it through this mess."

Like every sufferer, Paul's suffering exposes the depth of his weakness and the reality of his dependency. The question is, what will we do when suffering confronts us with the fact that independent, self-sufficient strength is a lie? Will we hoard our discouragement? Will we hide our weakness? Will we act as if we're okay when we're not okay? Will shame keep us from confessing what we know is true? Will we allow discouragement of heart to morph into despondency and maybe even paralyzing depression? Or will we reach out for the help that God has lovingly provided?

There's something else powerful about Paul's humble confession of weakness and heart desperation that's important to highlight. His despair isn't a prison; it's a doorway. Confessing that you don't independently have what's needed to walk through the travail on your plate is a gateway to receiving the care that only God can give you through the heart and hands of his people. Hopelessness is the doorway to hope. The confession of hopelessness frees you from attempting to do what you don't have the power to do on your own. The admission of hopelessness frees you from acting as if you're something that you're not. The confession of hopelessness robs shame of its paralyzing power. The confession of hopelessness frees you from isolation. The admission of hopelessness positions your heart to receive the gracious comfort that the God of all comfort has promised every one of his children.

Paul next reflects on the purpose of God in exposing the depth of our weakness. In the last two weeks of unrelenting pain and inability to eat or sleep, I have once again been comforted with the fact that it doesn't take much to shut me down and to make even the smallest of daily tasks virtually impossible. I'm faced with the fact that even on my strongest days, I am not independently strong. When I'm strong, it's easy to forget that my strength depends on God's constant provision and protection, without which I wouldn't be strong. Consider again the words of Paul: "But that was to make us rely not on ourselves but on God who raises the dead. . . . You also must help us by prayer." He's saying that his travail, in the hands of the Savior, becomes an instrument of grace.

The picture here is that every child of God has a warehouse of comfort, rescue, strength, wisdom, direction, and protection. But because of the pride and self-sufficiency that sin produces in us, we don't open the door of that warehouse; we live self-reliant lives, trusting that we can make it through on our own. So as an act of redeeming love, God leads us into situations that cause us to be confronted with our weakness so that we'll open the door to the lavish resources of help that are in his warehouse of grace. This week I have reached out to Eric, Bill, Alan, Malcolm, Steve, Rechab, DC, Shelby, Ben, Matt, Jeff, and Cheryl. These people have made the invisible help of the heavenly Father visible. They really have been the look on God's face, the sound of God's voice, and the touch of God's hand. They have spoken lovingly into the depths of my discouragement. They have lovingly confronted my fear. They have reminded me once again that I'm not alone. In ways that are hard to describe, they have given me strength to face the next day.

My physical situation hasn't changed; the pain and weakness are still there and might be there for a long time. But because of their willingness to incarnate God's grace, I have changed. I'm not giving in to weakness, wallowing in self-pity, and wasting my time worrying about the future over which I have no control. I'm right now doing what God has called me to do. I'm doing my best to put gospel words down on the page so that through my weakness and the comfort I've received from God's people, others too will be helped.

I have to stop and talk about my dear wife, Luella. No one in my life has more powerfully incarnated God's presence and provision. She always greets my fear, discouragement, questions, and complaints with amazingly patient grace, and she never fails to preach the gospel to me in my moments of amnesia and also to live the gospel before me. She stands as a rich blessing of mercy that I could never have earned or deserved. She's never too busy;

she's never irritated when I'm weak; she never pushes me to get my act together; she's always ready to complicate her life to give me the help I need. She's made it easy for me to confess things that are hard to confess and to be willing to receive what can be hard to receive. She is God's constant reminder that I have not been nor ever will be alone.

Second Corinthians 1, 1 Corinthians 12, and Colossians 3:12–17 tell us that God has never required any of his children to make it on their own. They remind us that we shouldn't be ashamed of our frailty. They assure us that God isn't disgusted by our lack of independent strength. Rather, they preach the gospel of God's sympathetic understanding, his faithful care, and his provision of the help we need in the presence and help of his people. There's comfort in the people of God. It won't be perfect. Nothing is perfect this side of eternity. But the messy resources of help from the people of God are a glorious comfort and provision to all God's suffering children.

There is one more thing that my friend TobyMac so wonderfully captured with these words: "What does it look like to admit your need and open the door to God's warehouse of provision?" Consider these steps.

1. Don't Suffer in Heroic Isolation

There's nothing noble about bearing down and suffering alone. In fact, it's a recipe for disaster. Everyone has been designed by God for community. Healthy, godly living is deeply relational. Worshipfully submissive community with God and humble dependency on God's people are vital to living well in the middle of the unplanned, the unwanted, and the unexpected. The brothers and sisters around you have been placed in your life as instruments of grace, and as I've said before, they won't be perfect instruments, they won't always say and do the right things, but in the messiness of these relationships God delivers to us what only he can give.

In my own suffering I've had to fight with the temptation of self-imposed isolation. There are times when I don't want to rehearse again what I'm going through. There are times when it seems too much to be around people. There are times when I've been hurt by the response of another and don't want to deal with that hurt again. At the same time, I'm convinced that it's important that I fight the isolation temptation. I know I need the presence and voices of others in my life who can say and do things for me that I could never do for myself, and I know that the relationship I have with these people is God's gift of comfort, rescue, protection, and wisdom. *Are you suffering in isolation?*

2. Determine to Be Honest

The first step in seeking and celebrating the gift of the comfort of God's people and experiencing how they can make the invisible grace of God visible in your life is to honestly communicate how you're handling what you're going through. Notice that I was careful in characterizing what you should communicate. Honest communication is not detailing the hardship you're going through and letting all the people around you know how tough you have it. Complaining tends to drive people away and to attract you to other complainers, which is far from healthy and helpful. Rather, every sufferer needs to be humbly honest about the spiritual battle underneath the physical travail so that brothers and sisters around you can fight that spiritual battle with you. If you're beaten down with an endless catalog of "what ifs," talk about it. If you're struggling with doubt about God, talk about it. If you're defeated by envying the lives of people who seem to have it better than you, talk about it. If you're discouraged by how long you've suffered, talk about it. If you feel that no one hears your prayers, talk about it. If you think that no one really understands your suffering, talk about it.

I'm not counseling you to buttonhole everyone you meet, but take advantage of the people in your life whom you are sure know and love you and know and love God. They are tools of right-here, right-now grace. Invite them to be warriors with you in the spiritual battle. And don't worry about what people think of you. Remember, you don't get your identity, peace, security, and rest of heart from them but from your Lord. No one in your life is capable of being your messiah; people are tools in the hands of your Messiah, Jesus. It would be impossible to fully communicate the depth of the comfort, strength, and counsel I have gotten at crucial moments of spiritual battle from the dear ones God has placed in my life. *Are you humbly and honestly communicating to others about how you're handling your hardship?*

3. Let People Interrupt Your Private Conversation

There's someone you talk to all the time about everything in your life. The opinions, interpretations, responses, beliefs, biases, perspectives, and viewpoints of this person are incredibly important and influential. You can't escape these conversations, and you can't avoid their influence. Most of the time, you're unaware that you're talking to this person, and most of the time you fail to realize how these conversations influence the way you think about yourself, God, others, and life. You've probably already guessed what I'm about to say—that person is you.

You have incredible influence over you, because no one talks to you more than you do. The problem is that there are times when it's very hard to say to ourselves what we need to hear. The travail of suffering is clearly one of those times. It's hard then to give yourself the hope, comfort, confrontation, direction, wisdom, and God-awareness that every sufferer desperately needs. So you need voices in your life besides your own. You

need to invite wise and loving people to eavesdrop and interrupt your private conversation, providing in their words things
you wouldn't be able to say to yourself. And don't take offense
when they fail to agree with your assessments; you need these
alternative voices. They're not in your life to hurt your feelings
but to give you what you won't be able to give yourself, and that
in itself is a sweet grace from the hand of God. *Who have you
invited to interrupt your private conversations?*

4. Admit Your Weakness

Doing well in the middle of hardship is not about acting as if
you're strong. God's reputation isn't honored by our publicly
faking what isn't privately true. The grave danger to sufferers is
not admission of weakness but delusions of strength. You see, if
you tell yourself and others that you are strong, then you won't
seek and they won't offer the enabling and strengthening grace
that every sufferer needs. And remember, the most important
form of weakness that we all face isn't the physical weakness
that accompanies so much of our suffering but the weakness of
heart in the midst of it.

I'd like to be able to say that the weakness I've had to deal
with in my suffering has been only physical, but that's just not
true. God has used my travail to expose weaknesses of heart that
I had no idea were there. He hasn't done that to shame me but
to create in me a desire for his transforming grace. I've learned
that nothing good ever happens when I deny weakness, and that
all kinds of good happens when I confess it.

Determine to be honest about your weakness, and in so doing,
invite others to be God's tools of his empowering and transforming grace. When you suffer, you view weakness either as an enemy
or as an opportunity to experience the new potential that is yours
as God's child. *Is your habit to admit or deny weakness?*

5. Confess Your Blindness

This side of eternity, since sin still lives inside us and blinds us, there are pockets of spiritual blindness in all of us. We all like to think that our view of ourselves is accurate, but in light of what the Bible says about the power of sin to deceive, we have to give up on the thought that no one knows us better than we know ourselves. As you walk through your travail, there may be inaccuracies of belief, subtle but wrong desires, wrong attitudes, susceptibilities to temptation, wrong views of others, struggles with God, and evidences of hopelessness that you don't see. So in love, God has placed his children in your life to function as instruments of seeing. They offer to you insight that you wouldn't have by yourself. Because they can see what you don't, they can speak into issues in your life, and by so doing be not only instruments of seeing but also God's agents of rescue and transformation.

Your need for these instruments of seeing shouldn't make you ashamed, as if there's something wrong with you. We all need these people, and we'll continue to need them until sin is no more and its power to deceive has been finally defeated. As you suffer, either you will be defensive when someone points out something you don't see, or you'll be thankful that God has placed people in your life, and you'll welcome them.

It's humbling but true of every sufferer that accuracy of personal insight is the result of community, because sin makes personal insight difficult. Since we all have areas where we fail to see what we need to see, we need to welcome those whom God has sent into our lives to correct and focus our vision. *How open are you when those near you help you see things in yourself that you don't see?*

6. Seek Wise Counsel

It's dangerous to make important life decisions in the midst of the tumultuous emotions and despondency of suffering. Often in the middle of hardship, it's hard to see clearly, to think accurately, and to desire what's best. The shock, grief, and dismay of suffering tend to rattle the heart and confuse the mind. If you're in the midst of wavering emotions and finding it difficult to have clarity of thought, it's dangerous to make in isolation the many decisions you'll have to make.

When you are suffering, you need to humbly invite wise and godly counselors into your life. I'm not talking here about professional help, although that's good if necessary. I'm talking about identifying the wise and godly people already in your life who know you and your situation well, who can provide the clarity of advice, guidance, and direction that is very hard to provide for yourself. Don't be threatened by this; it's something we all need, and wise sufferers welcome it and enjoy the harvest of good fruit that results. *Have you invited wise and godly counselors into your life to help you decide what would be hard to decide on your own?*

7. Remember That Your Suffering Doesn't Belong to You

Take time again to read 2 Corinthians 1:3–9. The message of this passage is clear: our sufferings belong to the Lord. He will take hard and difficult things in your life and use them to produce good things in the lives of others. This is one of the unexpected miracles of his grace. When it seems that my life is anything but good, God picks it up and produces what's very good in the life of another. Every sufferer needs to know that the comfort of community is a two-way street. Not only do you need the comfort of God's people, but your suffering positions you to be a uniquely sympathetic and insightful tool of the same in the lives of others.

Because of what you've gone through, you know what's helpful and what's not. You know when to speak and when to listen. You know where comfort is needed and when it's time to confront. You know how to lovingly break through anger and defensiveness. You know what it's like to feel hopeless. Your suffering has given you a toolbox of gospel skills that make you ready and equipped to answer God's call to be an agent of his comfort in the lives of fellow sufferers. God calls you not to hoard your suffering but to offer it up to him to be used as needed in the lives of others. And there's blessing in taking your eyes off yourself and placing them on others, because it really is more blessed to give than to receive. *Have you hoarded your suffering, or seen it as a means for bringing to others the good things that you have received?*

Yes, it's true that the God of all comfort sends his ambassadors of comfort into your life. They're sent to make God's invisible presence, protection, strength, wisdom, love, and grace visible. So welcome his ambassadors. Be open to their insight and counsel. Confess your needs so that God's helpers can minister to those needs. Live like you really do believe that your walk through hardship is a community project, and be ready for the good things God will do.

Review and Reflect

1. What temptations do you tend to face during your times of suffering?

2. In what ways do you communicate about your suffering? After reading this chapter, what new ways would you like to use?

3. Paul Tripp writes, "God makes his invisible grace visible by sending people of grace to give grace to people who need grace" (pp. 190–91). Who has God sent into your life for this very purpose? Take time to praise him for these people.

4. How is despair a doorway rather than a prison?

5. Paul lists several ways to open ourselves more to God during our suffering. In which of these do you need to be more willing? Prayerfully ask God to show you.

Heart Reset

- 1 Corinthians 1:18–31

- 2 Corinthians 1:8–11

- Colossians 3:12–17

14

The Comfort of a Heart at Rest

Suffering is the intersection where life's deepest pains meet with the most wonderful blessings of grace. It's the ground where mournful cries echo alongside heartfelt praise. It's the place where God seems absent and his presence is most clearly seen. It's the location of deep aloneness mixing with awareness of glorious love. It's the place of raging spiritual war and miraculous peace. Suffering is where weakness intersects with strength, confusion intersects with wisdom, sorrow intersects with joy, and despair intersects with hope.

Suffering has a unique ability to expose inadequacies in all the places we tend to look for life, hope, identity, joy, peace, motivation, and our reason to continue. If you're looking horizontally for what can only be found vertically, suffering will pick your pockets and leave you empty. Suffering shocks you into admitting that no human being can give you life. It forces you to acknowledge that your job can't give you identity. It shakes you into the realization that your physical body isn't the center of your true strength. It requires you to acknowledge that rest of heart isn't found in financial stability. It confronts you with the fact that personal peace doesn't come from what people think of you.

Perhaps this is one of the reasons that suffering is so painful. Suffering slaughters all our subtle God replacements. It exposes their utter inability to deliver what we're asking for. We live then with the pain and dismay of how quickly they're gone. We're left mourning, calculating the size of our loss. But we're not just mourning the person or the thing lost; the deeper mourning is the loss of what we were asking that person or thing to give us. In the face of losing what got us up and held us there, we wonder how in the world we're ever going to be able to continue. It's right then, in the darkness of our aloneness, loss, and fear, that the light of the gospel of God's presence and grace shines most brightly. It's one of the most profound paradoxes of life, that out of the darkest travail glorious beauty shines.

Tragedy and Beauty

No passage captures how beautifully rest and peace of heart can live in the middle of the unwanted, the unthinkable, and the unplanned hardships of life like Habakkuk 3:17–19:

> Though the fig tree should not blossom,
>   nor fruit be on the vines,
> the produce of the olive fail
>   and the fields yield no food,
> the flock be cut off from the fold
>   and there be no herd in the stalls,
> yet I will rejoice in the LORD;
>   I will take joy in the God of my salvation.
> GOD, the Lord, is my strength;
>   he makes my feet like the deer's;
> he makes me tread on my high places.
>
> To the choirmaster: with stringed instruments.

Few passages in the Bible are more important and encouraging than this passage, but you have to understand that it was written in the context of an agriculturally based economic system. If the fig tree, olive trees, and fields have completely failed, and all the livestock are gone, then there's been total cultural and economic devastation. There's nothing left. There's nowhere to look for help and hope. You couldn't find a scarier picture of hardship and loss. Yet in the middle of this horror, the prophet speaks of joy, of strength, and of leaping like a deer.

You can explain the stark contrast of total devastation and heartfelt joy in only one of two ways. Either the prophet is in complete denial of the inescapable, widespread loss around him, or he has learned something deeply healing and restorative that every sufferer desperately needs to know. Clearly the prophet isn't in denial but has come to understand life-altering truths rooted in the existence, presence, and power of God. These truths aren't impersonal, abstract items on some dusty theological outline. They're God's gracious gift to all his children as they encounter the difficulties of life, difficulties that no one is able to escape. These truths brim with life and hope at street level, where we all live and suffer. Let's consider the hope-giving lessons that are embedded in this wonderful passage.

1. Suffering Is Not Ultimate; God Is

The ultimate, eternal creator and controller of all things is God and God alone, and nothing exists outside the protective umbrella of his wisdom, power, and authority. God existed before his creation, and he'll live with eternal power after the world as we know it is gone. The hard things we face are neither eternal nor ultimate. No suffering lasts forever, and no suffering is the lord over our life. What may seem to have controlling power over us does not. What feels as if it will last forever won't. This means that even in the deepest, darkest suffering, there's hope and help to be found because God is bigger and more power-ful than any awful thing we will ever face. Because this is true, Habakkuk can rejoice even in the midst of economic ruin.

2. Difficulty Doesn't Control Your Fate; God Does

When we're going through hardship, it seems that we're under its control. It seems to be the lord over your schedule, finances, decisions, strength, and relationships. When we're in the throes of suffering, it feels as if an evil master has entered our house, bringing pain and chaos with him. But this passage reminds us that suffering doesn't control and determine our future; God does. The prophet chose his words carefully here. He could have called God many things, but he announces him as "the God of my salvation." Habakkuk is saying that our destiny is not deter-mined by the disasters around us. Rather, any present help and any future hope are in the hands of God alone.

It is wonderful and life changing to know that we're not con-trolled nor is our life determined by what we suffer but by the One who rules all the situations, locations, and relationships where that suffering takes place. Salvation isn't found in our ability to escape suffering but in the presence and grace of the One who meets us in it. This is why the prophet can have joy in the middle of such devastation.

3. Hardship Doesn't Define You; God Does

It's easy and quite normal to take on our difficulty as our identity. Divorce is a shocking and sad experience, but it isn't our identity. Systemic racism is horrible and demeaning, but as powerful as it is, it does not define you. Being continually bullied is a hardship difficult to bear, but it's not an identity. Whether it's the loss of a loved one, the betrayal of a friend, physical sickness, or financial ruin, no hardship in this fallen world has the power to define you or determine your potential. When you take what you've suffered as an identity, you tend to restrict your hope and potential to the confines of that experience, and in so doing you trouble your own trouble.

It is one thing to say, "I'm depressed," but quite another to say, "I am a child of the King of kings and Lord of lords, and I struggle with depression." This is why the prophet says, "GOD, the Lord, is my strength." He's saying that his power and potential aren't determined by his hardship but by his relationship to God, who not only created and controls all that is, but who has also promised to never forsake his children. This is why Habakkuk can speak with such hope when it seems there's no hope to be found.

4. What Will Truly Satisfy and Give Rest to Your Heart Cannot Be Taken Away

Here is the bottom line of what Habakkuk communicates and what this book is about. It's the only reason, in the middle of my own travail, that I would have the courage to write a book about the painful hardships that touch all our lives between the "already" and the "not yet." It's the thing that gets me up in the morning, infuses me with joy as I put it down on the page, and gives me rest of heart as I close my eyes to sleep. It's what I've grabbed hold of again and again when my suffering seems too hard to bear. It's what I long for others to get hold of as well. It's the message that I pray my life would preach. It's the most beautiful and practically helpful thing you could ever come to understand. If you get it, it will fundamentally transform the way you suffer. It will make your life an intersection where sorrow and joy meet. It will comfort you when there seems to be no comfort, and it will fill you with hope when it seems that all your hopes and dreams have died. To come to know this is much better and more beautiful than to live free of suffering. It's an honor and joy to be able to write these words with confidence. I hope you will let them sink in and settle in your heart. The one thing that will bring peace, joy, rest, and lasting satisfaction to your heart, nothing or no one can take away. In fact this thing is not a thing at all; it's a person, the Lord himself, who enters your life by grace and who will never, ever go away. When you find your hope and satisfaction in him, not in people, possessions, money, success, or physical health, no pain or loss can take that satisfaction away. When you truly place your hope in him, nothing is able to plunder your hope. When he holds your identity, nothing in life is able to rob you of meaning, purpose, and potential. His presence, power, and grace change everything. No wonder the prophet had joy in the midst of misery.

Here is the comfort for every sufferer: hope is a person, and his name is Jesus. Life is a person called Emmanuel. God enters your life by grace and by grace makes you the place where he dwells. So he goes wherever you go; he's there with you in whatever you're facing, and he lovingly provides you with everything you need. You don't have to search for him; you don't have to wonder if or when he will come; you don't have to earn his presence. His presence with you has been purchased by his own blood. In your suffering he gives you the best of gifts, the gift of himself. To be in him and he in you is infinitely better than having an easy, predictable, trouble-free life. And if hardship has been the tool that forges in you an unbreakable trust of him, then your hardship hasn't been for naught.

My prayer for everyone who reads this book is that you would rest, knowing that the most important, wonderful, and life-giving thing you could ever experience, no one or nothing has the power to take away. God is with you in hope-giving, rest-producing grace, and he is simply never going away!

Where shall I go from your Spirit?
    Or where shall I flee from your presence?
If I ascend to heaven, you are there!
    If I make my bed in Sheol, you are there!

If I take the wings of the morning
>   and dwell in the uttermost parts of the sea,
even there your hand shall lead me,
>   and your right hand shall hold me.
If I say, "Surely the darkness shall cover me,
>   and the light about me be night,"
even the darkness is not dark to you;
>   the night is bright as the day,
>   for darkness is as light with you.

For you formed my inward parts;
>   you knitted me together in my mother's womb.
I praise you, for I am fearfully and wonderfully made.
Wonderful are your works;
>   my soul knows it very well.
My frame was not hidden from you,
when I was being made in secret,
>   intricately woven in the depths of the earth.
Your eyes saw my unformed substance;
in your book were written, every one of them,
>   the days that were formed for me,
>   when as yet there was none of them.
How precious to me are your thoughts, O God!
>   How vast is the sum of them!
If I would count them, they are more than the sand.
>   I awake, and I am still with you. (Ps. 139:7–18)

Review and Reflect

1. Since suffering isn't forever for the Christian, how can you look
   at it in a more practical way?

2. What difficulty have you given too much power in your life?

3. What is defining you instead of God?

4. How do you need to rewrite your situation without denying it?

5. How has this book encouraged you about God and his character?

Heart Reset

- 2 Samuel 22:20

- Psalm 139:7–18

- Habakkuk 3:17–19

General Index

Scripture Index

PAUL TRIPP MINISTRIES

Paul Tripp Ministries connects the
transforming power of Jesus Christ to
everyday life through encouraging articles,
videos, sermons, devotionals, and more—
all available online and on social media.

PaulTripp.com

 /pdtripp   @paultripp   @paultrippquotes